AR

TIMBER BARONS:
Privilege & Scandal

outskirts
press

Timber Barons: Privilege & Scandal
All Rights Reserved.
Copyright © 2018 Arvin F. Spell, III
v4.0

The opinions expressed in this manuscript are solely the opinions of the author and do not represent the opinions or thoughts of the publisher. The author has represented and warranted full ownership and/or legal right to publish all the materials in this book.

This book may not be reproduced, transmitted, or stored in whole or in part by any means, including graphic, electronic, or mechanical without the express written consent of the publisher except in the case of brief quotations embodied in critical articles and reviews.

Outskirts Press, Inc.
http://www.outskirtspress.com

ISBN: 978-1-4787-9296-3

Cover Photo © 2018 Arvin F. Spell, III. All rights reserved - used with permission.

Outskirts Press and the "OP" logo are trademarks belonging to Outskirts Press, Inc.

PRINTED IN THE UNITED STATES OF AMERICA

*This book is dedicated to my dad
who shared many great family stories with me.*

Author's Note

In Appling County Georgia the longleaf pine trees grow tall; their sap runs rich. The sandy soil ranges from dark brown to black, sort of like the crickets that sing at night. My family's southern roots run deep through in it. This book is part of their story. Although most of the folks in it have passed, we southerners do protect our familial privacy, so all the names have been fictionalized to respect any relatives still living as well as to avoid positive identification of the characters.
It keeps the peace that way and promotes tranquility.

Arvin F. Spell, III
Boxwood House LLC

Table of Contents

Photographs I
One: The Community 1
Two: Ada 5
Three: Getting a Date 8
Four: Bad Trouble 14
Five: Things Get Ugly.. 20
Six: Married Life 24
Seven: Changing Times 33
Eight: Lillie 39
Nine: Big News 43
Ten: Ruined 46
Eleven: Everything Boils Over 49
Twelve: Big Changes.. 54
Thirteen: Divorce... 60
Fourteen: Adjusting... 65
Fifteen: New Beginnings... 72

Sixteen: Growing Pains 76
Seventeen: New Girl 78
Eighteen: Smitten 82
Nineteen: First Date 85
Twenty: Big Development 89
Twenty One: Getting Crowded 93
Twenty Two: Medical Emergency 98
Twenty Three: Busy Season 102
Twenty Four: Heir 108
Twenty Five: Explosion 111
Twenty Six: End of a Dynasty 113
Acknowledgments 117

Collecting Sap For Turpentine

Wikipedia/American Forestry Collection

Example of Turpentine Still 1909

Wikipedia/American Forestry Collection

Examples of Early 1900s Sawmill Operations

commons.wikimedia.org

Typical 1880—1900 Rural Home Timber Baron/Affluent Land Owner

Farm Buildings

Garage

Outhouse

Mule Barn With Corn Crib Behind

Author's Photographs

Example of Commissary /Naval Store Office

Example of Pack House That Could Have Masonic Lodge Upstairs

| VII

ONE

The Community

The 1800s were coming to a close, the page about to turn to a new century. For my relatives in southern Georgia it was a period of booming timber harvests and turpentine production. Their southern comforts as well as their southern dramas were in full swing, and I grew up hearing all the stories.

Timber interests and turpentine production, which resulted in the thriving naval stores industry, were the driving forces of most of the rural wealth. While farming was still important, timber and turpentine were the mainstays of the large landowners in the piney woods of central South Georgia. (Note: Naval stores were called such because pre-20th century they were businesses built exclusively around pine pitch/tar harvesting, the products used for caulking and water-proofing the old wooden ships and sailing tackle.) This area of Georgia was not a land of cotton and plantations before "the war."

Now we know there was only one war in the South, that little old disturbance between the North and the South over states' rights, so the all say. Well, after there were no more slaves, there were still workers and landlords with plenty of authority to keep the laborers in a situation that was still a society of class where all were not created equal, where all did not, shall we say, end up with equal slices of the

| 1

pie.

There were three classes of this society – landowners, poor whites, and Negroes who were at the bottom of the ladder with little hope of rising above that level. Additionally, there were strata of the classes, well defined by the groups themselves as well as by society in general. The people of the various classes lived together in largely self-sufficient rural communities. An example of a thriving, growing turpentine and naval store operation in this remote area of South Georgia during this period in history was Harton Place.

The main house was large, 8000 to 9000 square feet including the porches, Victorian in style, constructed by Mr. Harton somewhere between 1888 and 1890. It had twelve rooms including a large parlor with a bay window which jutted out beyond the porch. In fact, this window was the first thing you saw when you approached the front of the house. Undoubtedly, Mr. Harton intended that it should be a focal point since the top of the window was stained glass and was the only one in that part of the county. It was brought up from Savannah and had come by boat from New York, quite a show of wealth for an inland country area.

A large central hall ran from the front of the house all the way to the back porch and the kitchen. The porch itself wrapped three sides of the house which helped keep the rooms a little cooler in the hot and sultry summer weather. There was a vast dining room furnished with a spacious table which could seat a family of eight as well as anybody else who might show up at mealtime. Next to the kitchen a generous pantry housed copious ingredients for cooking. Off the kitchen was a small room where the cook, who was black, ate, along with any other black folks who might be present at meal time. (Note: Historically, this was the period when blacks did not eat at the table with the whites and were not even allowed to eat from the same dishes.) The rest of the house consisted of bedrooms, one of which was set aside for a sewing room and another for a study. A third room was

Mr. Harton's private domain where he could conduct undisclosed business, and where he kept a bottle of liquor or moonshine ready for himself or to share with his male visitors.

On this farm was a commissary which also served as the office for the naval store operations. The commissary sold everything required by farm residents except those items that were made on the farm. The store carried overalls, shoes, tobacco, mule collars, plow points, and single and double trees depending on whether one mule or two mules pulled the wagon or plow. Since the women generally made most of the clothes, the store also carried thread, needles, thimbles, cloth, and ribbon. Items that were not stocked could be ordered from the drummer, a traveling salesman, who made regular rounds in the region. Sometimes, rather than having to order a particular item, the drummer might happen to have it on the wagon when he came by the big house where he stayed a day or two since there was no lodging except with a family. One or two bedrooms were always available for visitors, it not being uncommon to have two beds in one room since the number of overnight guests who might appear at any one time was an unknown.

The drummer also always brought special treats for the children; one was store bought candy, a highly prized favor. At Christmas time when he brought fruit for the store to sell, he also brought fruit for the children at the big house as well as a peppermint stick close to a foot long.

In the late 1800s there was not yet a rural mail carrier going from farm to farm, so the store also served as a post office. The mail came once a week, having been collected in town or sent out with someone going in that direction. Of course there were no telephones yet, and if one wanted to send a telegram, doing so required a trip into town.

In addition to the commissary, this rural community where Harton Place was located had a cane mill, a sawmill, a cotton gin, a gristmill, and later on a turpentine still. All of these were for use by the big farm, but they also served the community because they could be used by smaller farmers or landowners for a fee or a share of what was being processed. Their use might also be put on an account at the commissary where a bookkeeper kept up with such records. When crops were sold the debtor would settle up his account. These accounts could run for a full year since supplies were needed in the winter and crops were not harvested until the next fall.

So besides the Harton clan, who else inhabited this rural South Georgia community? Where did they come from?

The landowners came from other parts of the South, usually from North Carolina or South Carolina, where they had been piney woods farmers on what was a frontier before the Civil War. They were small farmers who were predominately self-sufficient. Also, after the war, the larger landowners who were already in the south Georgia area, or who had migrated to the area with some means of acquiring land, journeyed to North and South Carolina where they talked to freed slaves about the opportunities in this rural area. The potential workers were promised a house and work for which they would be paid, and sometimes they were allowed to share in the profits made from their crops and labor. Since there was little work on the old plantations, and since most owners were too poor to pay them, many of these former slaves made an easy decision to move. Promises of work, a house, and food from the commissary for the winter, were better than anything they had.

This, then, was the world in which the Harton family lived. It was a life of relative comfort with many privileges for the upper class of this rural society. Jim Harton, the patriarch of the family, could trace his ancestry back to George Washington and the surrender of Cornwallis. The family had been among some of the early English settlers in North Carolina before relocating to Georgia. Jim's brothers owned small farms nearby, also in Appling County, having moved from Emanuel County where their grandfather had received a piece of land in a land lottery for Revolutionary War Veterans.

TWO
Ada

Of Jim Harton's eight children, four were still at home. The others were already married and lived on small farms of their own, but they were still closely tied to their father by needs of his mills and commissary. Ada was the oldest daughter still at home. At sixteen, having finished the seventh grade, it was time to think about finding a husband. However, she did not have any interest in the eligible prospects from the families they saw at church on Sunday, but then, youth being what it is, it was only a matter of time before a young man caught her eye.

To preface this piece of my story, I need to digress and say a bit about the turpentine business. Removing the sap from the pine trees for turpentine and rosin had become quite lucrative, and was a big part of Horten Place business. To capture the sap, trees were cut with a V-shaped instrument called a "hack," weighted on the bottom end to help with the cutting of the bark and tree to make the sap run. This work was done by both blacks and whites. In order to assure that the trees were being cut, Jim Harton had employed a "woods rider" to inspect the work each week. The woods rider he had employed was only eighteen. At the time he had just a first grade education, being forced to drop out of school to help support his brothers, sisters and mother as they only had a small farm. He rode on horseback to accomplish his duties, hence the job title of Woods Rider. He was a stately figure on horseback with riding boots, pants with suspenders, and a work shirt.

One splendid afternoon Ada came down to the commissary for a bottle of Uncle Drew's cane syrup and some other things. The clerk, Willis Johnson, got them up for her and put them on the counter.

Ada said, "My, that's a lot to carry, Uncle Arthur." Uncle Arthur, one of Jim Harton's brothers, was the bookkeeper, and he also managed the commissary.

"Well let me see," he said. "Asa, could you tote that up to the house for Miss Ada? I need Willis to sweep up before closing."

Ada liked this turn of events. They walked up the lane to the house, and as they arrived at the back steps to the kitchen, her mama came out.

"Child what is all that?"

"Stuff Lucille needs for cooking and asked me to go for."

"Mama, this is Asa Stall, Pa's woods rider, and he was kind enough to carry this stuff back for me."

"I see," said Mama. "Well put it in the kitchen."

Ada followed Asa in and politely said, "Thank you. Would you like a glass of buttermilk? Lucille just brought it up from the spring?"

"Yes, that'd be good –and please, a piece of cold cornbread if you have it."

Lucille said, "Right here in the top of the food safe." She opened the safe, a screened cabinet used for food storage to keep flies off the food, took out the plate, and cut off a piece of the cornbread. She handed it to Asa on a saucer along with the glass of buttermilk.

Ada said, "I appreciate you fetching that up here for me. Why don't you sit on the porch and have your milk and bread?"

Ada went on into the dining room and peeped out the windows. *My, he was handsome.* In reality, he was just medium height with ordinary brown hair, but the riding boots made him look taller and more important.

When Asa finished his cornbread and milk, he returned the dishes to the kitchen and went down the steps and back to the commissary to get his horse which he had left hitched there. On the way home he thought about Ada. *She was right pretty, and she seemed to be nice but she was Mr. Harton's daughter. Maybe I could just inquire and see if she's spoke for.*

Sometime after this, Ada saw Asa at a church social playing in a band made up of the local young men. She had not realized before that he was her father's woods rider, but now that she knew this, she decided it was time to get his attention. When Tuesday evening came around, she made an excuse to go to the commissary about six to get some vanilla extract for Lucille; she told the cook to tell her mama she had asked her to go.

It was customary at the end of each day for Asa to stop by the commissary to report on the day's activities, so when Ada arrived, Asa Stall was already there talking to Uncle Arthur. Ada spoke, and both inquired as to her health today and asked what they could do for her. That's when she decided on the spur of the moment that she needed more than vanilla extract; she needed to get enough that it would have to be carried back to the house for her.

"Mama sent me to get a sack of flour, some grits and a bottle of vanilla extract," she said.

Asa carried the groceries up to the house for Ada again.

THREE

Getting a Date

After Asa carried the groceries for Miss Ada, he went home. It was a four room structure with a hall and a kitchen off the side of the back porch. During supper he casually mentioned to his ma that he had carried groceries up to the big house for Miss Ada.

"Ma, she's nice and not bad looking."

"You may as well get that off your mind, Son; you couldn't afford her if she'd have you."

To himself, Asa thought, *well I might just be able to one day. I ain't gonna be no woods rider all my life.* But he said nothing to his ma, as you did not disagree with her about much. Next day he went on to work, and as he went about his usual responsibilities, his thoughts about Ada faded.

On Thursday his brother asked him, "You takin' anyone to the sing out at Hollyford Church on Sunday afternoon?"

"Well, hadn't thought about it 'cause I gotta to practice with the band on Saturday evening over at the Lodge Hall. Next weekend, it's Family Day, and we have to get in a good practice before we play for that."

That Friday evening when it was time for a report on the week's work, Asa arrived at the commissary. When he came in, Uncle Arthur said, "Mr. Jim wants you to come up to the house to talk to you about some possible new workers and if we can use them."

As Asa came up the lane, he saw Mr. Jim sitting on the porch in his screened enclosure. Mr. Jim had hired Asa's cousin, Quitman, to build a screened enclosure on rollers that he could move from one end of the porch to the other to take advantage of the shade and breeze.

As Asa came up the steps, Mr. Jim came out and said, "Let's walk down to the spring for a little refreshment." Mr. Jim kept a jug of moonshine down at the spring in addition to the one in his private room at the house.

They walked on down to the spring. Mr. Jim reached into the water and pulled out the jug. He took a seat on the bench and looked at Asa.

"Want a sip?"

"No thank you. I'll just have a drink of water." Asa reached over and picked up the gourd dipper laying on a rock and dipped up some of the cool spring water.

"Asa, sit down. We have a chance to get two black families from down near Jessup to come to work for us. One has worked in a sawmill, and the other has worked turpentine. Old Paul Tidwell, the drummer, told me about them, but do we need 'em?"

Asa thought a minute. "Well, you got that land over near Hollyford Church. We could use another hand there to cup the turpentine, and they're always lookin' for somebody to help out at the sawmill. If they're wantin' to work, sure, we could use 'em. Do you want me to go for 'em next week?"

After a minute Mr. Jim said, "No you send Old Jim Frederick to get 'em. He ain't able to work much no more, and he can go and fetch 'em." Jim Frederick was born into slavery and had come to Mr. Harton from a South Caroling plantation. He helped out at the turpentine still, but was getting on up in his years.

"Okay," Asa replied. "I'll set about seeing to gettin' that timber cupped over there by Hollyford. That reminds me, Mr. Jim; there is a sing over there at the church on Sunday afternoon. Would it be okay if I ask Miss Ada to go to the sing with me?"

Mr. Jim looked a little stunned and took a swig out of his jug. To Asa it seemed like fifteen minutes must have passed before he replied. He said finally, "Who's going with you besides her?"

Asa had to think fast. He could say his ma, but she might not go so he said, "How 'bout her sister coming along, too?"

"Well, I think that'd be mighty fine, but you better come up to the house with me and ask her if she wants to go and if it's alright with her mama."

When they came up on the porch, Ada was setting the table for supper and through the lace curtains on the windows, she saw them coming.

Mr. Jim hollowed out, "Ada come out here a minute."

She came out. "Yes, Pa?"

"Asa has somethin' to ask you."

Asa turned red as a beet, but he stammered out, "Miss Ada, would you like to go to the sing Sunday afternoon over at Hollyford Church?"

Now it was Ada's turn to feel a little heat in her face. "Well, I guess so if it's okay with my pa and mama."

Mr. Jim said, "Go ask your mama, but your little sister, Trudie, has to go along for the ride."

Ada went inside and down the hall to her mama's room. Miss Jamie did not feel well and had a bad cough. When Ada told her about the invitation, she said, "Go ahead if it's okay with Pa, but Trudie must go, too."

Ada returned to the porch, all smiles. "I can go," she said. "What time should I be ready?"

Asa said, "'Bout 2:30. It's only two miles."

Ada left the men alone, and Mr. Jim said, "Asa, you know you're doing a good job as woods rider. Arthur tells me we are getting more tar than ever before now that the hands are keeping the boxes streaked on a regular basis. We're gonna have to add another still day before long to take care of what's coming in."

About this time Trudie came to the door and said, "Pa, supper's ready."

Mr. Jim said, "Asa, you stay to supper with us."

Asa thought and then said, "Thank you, Sir, but I best get on home. Ma will be expecting me and waiting my supper there."

Asa rode his horse on home, and when he got to the barn lot, he removed the saddle and bridle and fed the animal. Then he hurried up to the house and ran up the steps. Indeed, Ma was waiting supper on him. His pa wasn't around much because he was out hunting and fishing a lot, and Ma depended on Asa as the "man of the house" when Pa was away.

Ma asked, "What you in such high spirits about?"

"Well, Ma, Mr. Jim said I was doing an excellent job, and I asked Miss Ada to the sing on Sunday and she said yes." His ma just looked at him.

"I need the buggy Sunday to take her in, and her sister, Trudie, is going along, too."

Ma said, "Well, I don't know about all of this but I reckon it's okay."

Saturday morning Asa got up and did all the wood chopping for Ma. Then he saddled the horse and went off to the turpentine still to see that all the tar cupped yesterday was being brought in. The wagons were lined up to go up the ramp with their barrels of tar to be unloaded on the platform.

Let me take my readers aside here to describe the turpentine still. It was a two-story structure with a dirt ramp on one end. On the lower level were a furnace and a large kettle with an opening to the second

GETTING A DATE | 11

level where tar was poured out of the barrels for processing. Starting on the lower level, and going through to the second level, was a large wooden tub which held several hundred gallons of water and through which ran a circular copper coil that was connected to the large cooker. As the tar cooked, steam rose through the coil and was cooled by the water. That became liquid spirits of turpentine which then flowed out of the faucet at the bottom of the large barrel and was collected in large 50-gallon metal drums. The stiller had to pay attention to his "spirit" level to determine when the batch was done.

The filled drums were rolled into the "spirit room" until enough drums accumulated to transport them to town for sale. When the spirits were cooked off, the trough connected to the boiler was opened for the hot rosin to pour out into a vat. The vat was a V-shaped metal container over which a removable wire screen was placed. The screen was lined with batten, cheap batten which was a coarser grade of medical cotton. The batten captured all of the trash, chips and pine straw collected in the woods when the tar was dipped (taken from the collecting cups). What filtered through was clean rosin, which was a bright amber color. After the rosin had drained through the batten, the screen was removed and the hot rosin dipped into metal drums to be sold. When rosin was turned out in the vat, the smell of it permeated the air.

On top of the batten was a product called "dross," a mixture of the chips and rosin stuck together. When it cooled, the dross was chipped off and used to start fires as well as to keep the steam pumps running. These pumps moved water from the larger open well to the condensing barrel. At the end of the still day, the stiller had to make sure that the fire was completely out because the high flammable nature of the still products always presented an immense fire danger.

This flammable dross was used by many of the hands to start fires in their stoves or fireplaces. Uncle Jim always keeps some at the big house for Lucille to start the fire in the cook stove. In winter a bucket of it was kept by the woodpile for starting the fires in the fireplaces.

The batten was stored and about once a month a dealer would stop by and pay a little for it and haul it away.

Asa, as the woods rider, had a large responsibility in keeping the still operation busy. He had to make sure the trees were cut weekly, that the tree cups were emptied regularly, and that after the pine resin was collected, it was delivered straight away to the still. So, Saturday, after checking on the cupping process, Asa went by the commissary and picked up the small list of things his ma had asked for and went home. Then he went down to the creek where he took a bath and put on clean clothes before heading off to practice.

His mind wasn't much on the practice because he was thinking about the next day – the sing, his date with Ada, and what the future might bring – but he tried to concentrate on getting ready for next Saturday's Lodge picnic events.

The Lodge was a country Masonic Lodge known as Harton Lodge because of its location in the second story of a school house built by George Harton. He had been the first Master of the Lodge and was brother to Jim Harton. Most of the family men were members of the Lodge.

Asa's band practiced until about 9:00 when they felt they were ready for the picnic. Asa played the bass horn, and the group had decided he should do a solo backed by them. They let him choose what he wanted to play, and he chose *When You and I Were Young Maggie*. That song was his favorite. Some of the other boys would sing. Their program at the Lodge would last about an hour.

After practice finished, Asa headed for home which was about three miles. Everyone was in bed when he got there. In those days before electric lights, you got up early – at sunrise – and went to bed about sundown. Seeing by a kerosene lamp or candle was okay, but both candles and fuel needed to be saved, as they were expensive.

After Asa got into bed, he drifted off wondering what the next day and his date with Ada would be like.

GETTING A DATE | 13

FOUR

Bad Trouble

Sunday morning dawned bright as a new penny. Asa's ma was up before day break and in the kitchen fixing breakfast. On this morning she had made biscuits and fried up fatback. Since the hens had been laying well, there were fresh eggs, and she cooked some grits.

Asa came in the kitchen, and Ma said, "Breakfast's ready. Where's your brother and sisters? Go fetch 'em; they gotta get ready for church."

"Okay, but when I get back from the barn, I just want some cold cornbread and milk."

Eula Mae, Sally Ann, Mary Sue and Robert were Asa's sisters and brother. He'd hollered for them, and when they all came tromping in, Eula Mae asked, "Asa what's this I hear about you going to the sing with Ada Horton?"

"Well, it's true. I am," Asa said.

"Can me and Sally Ann come along?"

"No, her sister, Trudie, is going along with us."

With that, Asa went out to the barn to clean up the buggy and brush his horse. He wanted to cut a fine streak when he went to pick up Miss Ada. His mind was already working.

Shor'd be nice to be Mr. Jim Horton's son-in-law. Lord knows none of his own sons are very interested in the farming and naval stores operations. Each of 'em has a small farm and one of 'em is foreman at the saw mill. The others work at the cotton gin and grist mill, but none of 'em work with the turpentine operation. That could be my area. I'm already his woods rider, and there's a future in turpentine. Money to be made there. He smiled to himself.

These thoughts were interrupted when Sally Ann came in to milk the cow. "Asa, ya shore are spiffing up that buggy. Ya must be trying to make a real big impression on them Horton girls."

"Hush up, Sally Ann; it just needed a good cleaning."

Sally Ann went into the stall and got feed out for the cow. Then she sat down on the stool and began to milk. The process was going well until the cow switched her tail at a fly and hit Sally Ann in the face with a tail full of cockleburs. Sally Ann let out a yell and the cow stepped in the pail. Sally Ann grabbed the pail, saved the milk, and continued milking until she finished. Then she carried the pail up to the kitchen and put a flour sack over the edge to strain the milk, filtering out the trash from the cow's hoof and whatever else might have fallen in while she was milking.

Her ma said, "Give me that and y'all get dressed for church. You know the preacher comes today; it's second Sunday."

You see, in those times there were half-time and quarter-time preachers in the country churches because they could not afford a full-time preacher. The Stills went to the Freewill Baptist Church which was small and quarter-time. The Hortons went to the Southern Baptist Church which was half-time. Some of the other Still relatives went to Hollyford which was a half-time Church of God congregation.

Everybody got all dressed up and ready to go, the girls in their Sunday skirts and Sunday blouses with ribbons in their hair, and Robert with clean pants and shirt.

"Cause I ain't going today. I spect your pa be home any minute. He's been gone all week, and I jus' know he'll have a mess of fish, rabbits, and birds to be dressed and cooked."

"I'll stay home, Ma, and help out with the stuff Pa brings in," Asa volunteered.

As they climbed into the wagon to leave, Ma warned, "Robert, you behave and don't you dare spook that mule or get him out a trot, or I'll skin your hide when you get back." So off they went, Robert feeling awfully important to be driving his sisters to church.

They covered the three and a half miles to church and got there about 10:30, giving the girls some time to talk to other girls they hadn't seen in three weeks. About 10:45 the preacher come riding up in his buggy. Ms. Odie Mae Taylor cranked up the pump organ and played a song or two which meant it was time to go inside.

Brother Peoples was the preacher. He read the Bible and prayed, and then he preached. It was the usual sermon all about what would happen to you if you didn't live by the Ten Commandments and honor your father and mother and live a life according to the Bible. You would wind up in Hell when you died and burn forever. It was enough to scare you half to death. The way he painted such an awful picture of that fire you could practically feel the heat.

When he finished, he prayed, "If there be one here today let him come into the fold now before it's too late." The congregation sang the invitational hymn *Just As I Am*, but nobody moved.

When church was over Robert and the girls headed home. It was about one o'clock when they got back, and Asa was on the porch. "How was church?" he asked.

Without any enthusiasm Robert responded, "The usual hell fire and brimstone Brother Peoples always talks about."

Asa said, "Well, Pa's home, and he brought some fine rabbits."

Just then ma announced, "Dinner'll be ready quick as you change."

They all rushed in and got ready for dinner. Ma had cooked up rabbit stew and dumplings, fresh beans from the garden, and pickled beets.

Pa was worn out from hunting, and he was sleeping, so Ma told everybody, "Now y'all don't make lots of noise this afternoon. Your pa needs his rest."

The girls helped clean up the kitchen, then walked down to the creek.

Meantime Asa put on his Sunday best and a fresh shirt Ma had washed and ironed for him on Saturday. He borrowed his pa's coat which Pa rarely wore except to a funeral or the occasional wedding. When it was time, he went out to the barn, hitched up the buggy, and headed off to pick up Miss Ada, who by now he was figuring just might be his future bride, as he would like being married into the Horton family. After all, none of the Stills had what the Hortons had. The Stills only owned small farms of about sixty acres each, and Asa had bigger dreams.

The Hortons were in another position altogether. They owned more than 500 acres of cultivated land and over 2,000 acres of timber land. Asa thought to himself, *that's what I want, and I got to get a start somewhere.*

With so many thoughts tumbling through Asa's head, he arrived at the Horton home before he knew it. Mr. Jim was on the porch in his screened enclosure. Asa spoke as he came up the steps, and Mr. Jim told him, "Knock on the screen door to let 'em know you're here."

Asa did, and then Mr. Jim said, "Come sit down. They'll be out shortly. Did you go to church this morning?"

"No sir," replied Asa. "I stayed home to help Ma with what Pa brought home from hunting."

"Well now, I ain't been hunting or fishing in a while. My legs bother me when I walk a lot so I don't go much. ...So tell me; how do the crops look to you, Asa?"

"Well sir, what I've seen look good. The cotton's beginning to crack; the corn's drying. Won't be long 'til time to gather it all in."

Mr. Jim responded, "I hope that damn cotton gin don't stay busted all the time this year. That boy of mine, Lett, don't seem to be able to keep it running."

About this time, Ada came out followed by Trudie. "We're ready."

For Asa she was a sight to behold. She had on the prettiest blue striped dress with little pink roses in between and a bonnet to match. She had her light brown hair pulled back under the bonnet and tied at the back with a blue ribbon. "You look mighty pretty today, Miss Ada; umm, uh what I mean… well you always look fine."

Trudie chimed in, "And how about me?"

"Oh, you look fine too, Miss Trudie." Then he quickly added, "We better be off, or we'll miss the beginning of the sing." He helped Miss Trudie into the back of the buggy and Miss Ada up on the front seat. He clucked to his horse, and they were on their way.

When they arrived at Hollyford, Asa was in fine spirits. They had been able to carry on a steady conversation, and he was right proud to have the privilege of escorting Miss Ada to the sing. When he hitched the buggy and helped the girls down, they walked toward the church. He could hear the whispers.

"That's Jim Horton's girls with Asa Still." Asa had lots of kinfolk who went to Hollyford since their small farms were nearby. He felt sure they were impressed.

The sing got underway about 2:30. The Williams Sisters were up first and sang several songs including *Precious Memories*. Then there were several other singers including the Pearson Boys and Ella Mae Wooten who sang a solo, *In the Garden*. Most of the singers were from the Zora community in Appling County.

Things were moving along when about four o'clock, Reverend Hand interrupted and came up to the pulpit to make an announcement. Everybody figured it would be about future sings or services. Instead he said, "There has been a disturbance in the quarters over at the Johnson Place near Jim Horton's sawmill. It would be best if you all started for home so as to be in before dark."

That is all he said, giving no details as to what had happened.

Asa got the girls in the buggy and headed for home. They were back by five o'clock. Mr. Jim heard them coming, and before Asa could hardly tell Ada how much he had enjoyed her company and hoped to see her again, Mr. Jim was on the steps. Ada did manage to tell him he could stop by any time before her pa said, "Go inside girls. Asa and I need to talk."

"This afternoon about 3:30 one of the Ratkin Girls, who lives on Tommy Johnson's Place, was raped by a Negro. It seems she had walked down to the branch below their house, and he came out of the bushes and attacked her. Least wise that's what she told her paw. It wasn't one of our hands, and we're not sure who he was. My boys, the Quinn brothers, and some of the Johnson farmers are looking for him. You know them Ratkins are white low life, so no tellin' what really happened, but it's got the whole neighborhood in an uproar, and the word has already spread to town. Lord knows what's comin' next. You go on home, Asa; keep a watch out for this black fella."

Asa started for home, and on the way he stopped by Jim Frederick's house to see if he knew anything new.

"I, no Suh, I don't know nothin' about this. He ain't one of ours 'cause all of our young mens has been accounted for this afternoon. Me and Bub Blanden done check on all ours."

That was a relief to Asa and reassurance that it wasn't any of his turpentine hands that started this trouble. He hoped it would all be blown over by tomorrow since it was hard enough to get the crews to work on Monday morning without this sort of trouble.

BAD TROUBLE | 19

FIVE
Things Get Ugly

The ruckus had just begun over this rape. Word was out in town and all over the countryside that there had been a rape of a white woman by a Negro. Then it was being told more than one had been molested. The county sheriff had been contacted by Jim Harton, who had sent one of his boys into town. The sheriff sent back two of the county's blood hounds. About sundown you could hear them barking through the woods.

The sheriff said, "Tell the boys to bring the n****r in so we can lock him up."

The black man had not moved very far from the branch where it all happened. Until he heard the hounds baying, he had no idea anything was wrong. He knew he ought not to have messed with that white girl, but she was willing. In fact, she led him on, and he was afraid if he didn't go along, she would say he had molested her and get him in trouble. *Well*, he thought, *maybe she'd done told what happened anyway*.

He decided he had better move on and hide 'til morning and then be on his way. He had left Denton and was headed to Eastman to see if he could find work where his cousins had gone down to a timber operation in Dodge County when he got into this bad situation.

Looking around the area, the fellow saw the Harton turpentine still and decided he would hide in the wood pile that was stacked up for the furnace on the far side of it. He crept down in a pile of wood and went to sleep thinking everything would be all right and that he would be on his way before daylight.

About ten o'clock he was awakened by the dogs barking and pawing at the wood pile. It was too late to run. The men pulled down the wood and there was the prize.

"You black son of a bitch. We got you now. Who the hell you think you are molesting that white woman? Boy your ass is in big trouble. The sheriff's waiting to lock you up. Get up from there! On your feet you bastard! Where you from anyway, boy?"

The black man responded that he was from Denton on his way to Eastman. "I ain't done nothing to that girl 'cept what she wanted me to."

One of the Parson boys struck him with his shotgun and said, "Shut your mouth. Ain't no white woman wanted you touchin' her."

The black man began to whimper. "Lousy, sir, I be telling the truth. I ain't attack no white girl. I swear I only done what she wanted me to."

By this time they had drug him out of the wood pile and quieted the dogs. They tied his hands behind his back and were about to put him in the wagon to haul him into town when they heard horses coming. They looked around and there they were – the Ku Klux Klan.

Their leader said, "Boys, you done a fine job. We'll take him for you and see that he's taken care of."

Nobody argued. The Harton boys left to carry the dogs up to the house to feed. The Klan took the prisoner, strapped him on a horse, and headed for town. They got as far as the sawmill and stopped.

"String that n****r up! No need to waste the sheriff's and judge's time with the low life bastard. Get some rope, boys."

The black man let out a terrified yell. "I didn't do nuthin', boss, except what that girl wanted me to."

"No white woman wanted you; no matter even if she was trash. You took advantage of her being alone down at that branch. Now yur gonna pay. Here, boys, tie him to that tree with this roll of barb wire. Stuff his mouth so he can't holler. We wouldn' want the women folk to hear him yelping," the hooded speaker sneered.

The Klan tied him to the tree.

"Shoot the bastard, and let's go," one Klansman urged.

One of the others said, "No, let's castrate the son of a bitch and leave him. He won't be bothering nobody no more." He pulled out his knife. "He ain't no better than a hog."

Then they ripped off his pants. The captive squirmed, but to no avail as the barb wire cut into his flesh. They cut off his testicles and pulled up his pants. They left him like that and rode off. The next morning the Harton boys were on their way to carry the dogs back to town when they discovered the black man tied to the tree, the ground beneath him soaked in blood. He was dead.

They went up to the house and got Mr. Jim. Shaking his head, he said, "Cut him down and carry him to the sheriff."

The men cut him down, put him in the wagon, and hauled him to town. The sheriff called to the black man who worked for him and said, "Go bury the poor devil. The Klan's done my work for me."

This was the way crime involving a Negro was handled in the South for many years. There was no real justice, just conviction and punishment, often execution. Negroes were at the bottom of the social order and unless protected by a white landlord, stood little chance of a trial. The Klan used occasions like this to make an example for the other blacks to keep them in line, subservient. The prevailing attitude was a Negro was all right as long as he stayed in his place. To talk back to a white man would probably bring on a pistol whipping and a sharp reprimand. "Remember your place boy!"

So, given the times, the sheriff didn't bother to investigate. No one knew who was in the Klan except their members, and they would not talk. The boys who found the Negro at the still may have thought they knew who some of them were, but nobody would say if they did. It was the belief of the whites that, no matter how poor they were, they were still better than the Negros. It did not matter that some of them made no more money than the black hands or that they were just as dependent on the landlord. In the case of race they stuck together. It also didn't matter whether the Raskin girl encouraged the Negro or not. He was guilty and out of line to one and all. Even the blacks themselves said he had no business messing with that white girl.

The only thing Jim Harton told his wife and daughters was that they had caught the fellow and the sheriff was handling the matter. That was true in a way. He did not feel there was any need for them to hear the gory details.

When Asa came by the sawmill lot, Jim Harton came out, and Asa stopped and inquired, "What happened with the rape? Any news?"

"Well, they found him in the wood pile at the still and were takin' him into town to the sheriff when the Klan came along and took over. They finished him off over there by that tree. I just washed the blood away."

Asa thought to himself that there must be a better way to deal with the blacks than this, but he said nothing and went on to get started on cupping the acreage out at Hollyford.

SIX

Married Life

The days moved forward, and Asa continued to work for Jim Harton, learning all he could about the turpentine business, farming, and managing a large rural operation. In 1910 he asked for Ada Harton's hand in marriage. They were wed, and a year later a daughter, Elizabeth, was born, and then in 1915 a son was born – Asa Stall II (Asa Jr.).

When Asa married, he could not read or write, but since Ada was educated, she began teaching him both to read and to write. When he would go by the commissary in the evenings on the way home, he would copy some labels from cans and signs, and she would teach him what they were. Studying with her, Asa learned his letters and how to sign his name. He understood that acquiring this knowledge would help him achieve the goal of owning his own business.

The young family was living in one of Mr. Harton's houses which he had allocated to them when they married. It was comfortable enough but only four rooms, and the family was growing. Asa had saved up some money and decided it was time to own his own home and piece of land. On December 23, 1917, he purchased 75 acres of land for $1,500.00 from Jim Harton, now his father-in-law. It was about a mile from the main Harton spread. It had one field on it that was roughly twenty acres. The rest was virgin heart pine timber.

The deed to purchase the property was hand written in ink and the plat of the property drawn off on the bottom of the deed. No survey was done because all concerned understood the boundaries. Asa had saved enough money not only to buy the property, but to build a house as well.

In January when there was little work on the farm or in the woods, and the sawmill was not busy, Asa took the turpentine hands, cut 30 acres of the heart pine, and constructed a six room house with a central hall. The house was two rooms deep with the third room on each side extending beyond the two central rooms. These rooms were reached by passing through one of the other rooms. The front of the house was wrapped on three sides with a porch, and the rear of the house had a porch which extended the entire length of the back of the house. In the middle of the rear porch was a shed roof which extended to the well that was dug near the end of the porch. The casing for the well extended through the floor and had a shelf built around it. This shelf ran the entire length of the shed, and was called a water shelf. The rear kitchen door opened onto the porch, and water could be brought to the kitchen from the well which had a hand pump in it.

In the beginning the house was framed in with no partition walls. The inside was open except for the 2x4s which divided the rooms. The house had four brick fireplaces with board mantels and a flue in the kitchen for the wood stove. The windows and doors were ordered from Savannah, came by train to Hazlehurst, Georgia, and were brought out to the property by wagon. All of the windows were the same length including the ones in the kitchen. They were tall windows reaching almost to the floor. During the winter months Asa put up beaded ceiling boards in the central hall. This divided the house with two partitions; in other division of rooms, privacy was created by hanging sheets or quilts. Asa and Ada and their two children moved in March when the house was livable.

The front and rear doors were half glass with side lights. They opened to the front and rear porches at each end of the central hall. There was no indoor plumbing. The outhouse was in the back, a sufficient distance away to keep the smell from the house.

During the next year, Asa cut more lumber and partitioned the house off with rough 10" boards. The boards were then hung with cheese cloth and wallpaper was applied over this. The rest of the ceilings were done in beaded board, and the walls in the kitchen and dining rooms were finished with the beaded boards since this was more durable than wallpaper. Over the years the house was changed indicating the family's increasing wealth. The pillars on the porch were done in one-half brick with tapered rectangular posts above with square caps for tops. As money was available, the fireplaces were redone in brick with molded cut wood mantels.

In 1920 Asa was ready to go into business for himself with a partner – Lott Jenkins, a fellow land owner. Jenkins put up several hundred dollars for them to begin operation, and at the end of the crop sales in the fall, the business was able to repay the money advanced by Jenkins with enough left to run through the winter. This was an excellent start, and the business continued to grow each year.

When the house was pretty well finished, Asa began constructing his own commissary, and all that went with it, on the original 75 acres he had purchased. First a boiler shelter was constructed. This was a shed with a central section that was higher than the two sheds on each side of it. Toward one end was placed a big boiler which held a hundred gallons or more. It was made of iron in the shape of a huge bowl. Around this was constructed a brick and concrete enclosure with an opening and extension to hold a fire box. Logs were pushed in to heat the contents of the boiler. On the side was a brick smoke stack which went out above the roof to carry the smoke away. On the side next to the chimney, or sometimes the fire box, there was an opening where wood was stacked to dry. The shed on the opposite side had an enclosed room with a dirt floor for storage. These boilers were used for syrup boiling and hog killing, both important operations on these rural homesteads. In addition to the boiler building, Asa was also adding other buildings central to rural Georgia farm operations. These included a smokehouse where hams and sausage were cured and kept for winter months, a chicken house, and an ice house.

The ice house is of particular interest because of the way it was constructed. The exterior and interior walls were wood with the space between the walls filled with sawdust for insulation. The interior walls were lined with tin. The doors were double thick with sawdust insulation and tin lining. The ice house consisted of an upper and lower partition, the upper portion with a small door where large blocks of ice were slid in to keep the lower portion cool. These blocks of ice were delivered from town by the ice company on an ice truck. Essentially, this building was a big version of ice boxes in homes of the period.

By now Asa's operation had a cow barn, too. The cow barn was a large central two-story structure with two one-story shed extensions on each side. These were divided into stalls and one-quarter of one side was made into a corn crib and feed storage room. The upstairs of the two-story portion was used for hay storage. This barn was used for the milk cows. One or two were always kept to supply milk and butter for the family.

It was customary to keep a Holstein and a Guernsey. The two calved at about the same time, and when the calves were born, the cows began producing milk. The milk from the cows was mixed because the Guernsey milk was much richer and contained more cream than Holstein milk. Since this was not a dairy farm, the calves were left with the cows which were bred to beef bulls. The bulls were usually Whiteface Herefords, which produced offspring more in line with beef cattle.

Milking was a morning ritual. The cows were milked by hand with the milk going into pails. The pails with the milk and some trash off the cows were taken to the kitchen where the milk was strained. Some of the milk was put in pitchers in the ice house for drinking. The balance of the milk was poured into crockery bowls and placed on the screen enclosed milk shelf on the rear porch outside the back kitchen door. The milk was left there for the cream to rise to the top of the bowls. The heat during the day soured the milk and turned it to a semi-spoiled stage known as clabber. The cream was then skimmed off the top leaving the clabber.

Cream was placed in the butter churn to make butter. If you had a churn with a handle that turned wooden paddles you used that, or a family might have an earlier version of the crockery jar and stick type. If a family had neither, the cream was placed in a half gallon glass jar and someone rocked it over their knees until the cream turned to butter. When the butter was ready, it was spooned out of the churn into a dish.

To make the butter pretty, it could be packed into a wooden mold with a design cut in the wood and left to cool. To remove the butter from the mold there was a handle that was pressed down to release a round hunk of butter with a design on the top.

What was left in the churn was buttermilk. Some folks, like Asa, loved a glass of buttermilk with a hunk of cornbread. That buttermilk also made wonderful biscuits.

The clabber which was left in the bowls could be used for biscuits, but generally it wound up in the slop bucket, which was a container set out near the smoke house and which received all kitchen waste. The contents of this bucket were not fed to the dogs or chickens, but were mixed with wheat shorts and fed to the small pigs.

The mixture was poured into a V-shaped trough made of wood with cross pieces of wood to help prevent the pigs pushing each other away from the food. They would eat until they were so full they would just lay in the trough and sleep. Just when a pig was too big to eat this mixture was determined by an opening in the pig pen fence – whether the pig was too fat to get in and out through the opening.

Asa and Ada's kitchen of this period did not have built in cabinets. Instead, there was a work table with a shelf for pots and pans underneath. In the center of the kitchen was a large Home Comfort Range, the fanciest wood stove available at the time. It had a hot water tank on the side. The wood fire heated the water as well as the stove top for cooking. Above the stove top were "warming ovens" for keeping food warm after it was cooked. The baking oven was on the bottom. Maintaining a constant temperature was difficult as it just depended on the heat from the wood.

In addition to the stove there was a food safe, a cabinet with wire screened doors where food was placed after meals to keep the flies and insects off, items such as left over biscuits, cornbread and anything else from the mid-day meal. The mid-day meal, called dinner, was the big meal of the day. At night supper was often warmed up dinner with a few additions. Another essential item in the kitchen of this period was a Hoosier cabinet, which contained the flour bin and sifter and held spices and sugar for cake and pie baking.

Outside the expanding house, the farming operation was growing, too. As part of this growth, mules were needed for cultivating the land. They were the power which pulled the plow, the turpentine wagons and the log carts, all of which produced income for the business. They were very valuable assets and had to be cared for properly. Therefore, Asa constructed a mule barn across from his house, about 2,000 feet from the cow barn.

It was an extremely fine barn made out of lapped weather board just like the house. It had a large hay loft with permanent stairs up to it. The loft had openings in the side to push the hay out into the racks for the mules to eat. Behind the barn was a large corn crib since the mules were fed both corn and hay. The corncrib also served as corn storage for the other animals on the farm, and the corn crib and hay loft provided places for Asa's children to play. Digging peanuts out of the hay or having a corn cob war was great fun, or just climbing to the top of the crib and sliding down the corn. The barn was also a great place for a game of hide and seek.

By this time Asa had tenant farmers, persons who farmed the land of another paying rent with cash and/or a portion of the crops. The farmers lived in houses on the farms they cultivated. They were required to maintain the fences associated with the farm since the fences were meant to keep out the cows and hogs that were left loose to roam the woods.

These farmers also used Asa's mules. They checked them out in the morning at day break to go to their farms or to the woods to work. Asa required them to bring the mules to the barn every afternoon so he could be sure they were fed and cared for. This way he was sure the mules were well treated and not abused during the day by the farmers. Any cuts of lashes had to be explained.

With farming and turpentine operations growing, Asa enlarged the commissary. It was a building about 40 ft. long and about 20 ft. wide with a front porch on it. The inside was laid out in a "U" shape with counters around the central isle. In the front behind the counter was an enclosed wire cubicle where the bookkeeper sat at a roll top desk. Some cash was paid for items, but most of the business was "charge account." The farmers then paid their bills when the crops were sold. The turpentine hands paid their bills weekly except during the winter when they had little or no work so they were given until spring to pay up their accounts.

Behind the counter in the rear of the store was a suspended frame of boards held up by chains. The flour and meal were kept up there so the rats would not get into the merchandise. There were wood bins for rutabagas, potatoes, and onions. There was a salt box under the counter where cured fat back was kept. Hoop cheese was also in this area. On the counter were scales to weight the fatback and cheese. The farmers and turpentine hands came in on Friday afternoon or Saturday morning to get their orders filled for the next week's supplies.

In 1925 when Jim Harton died, Asa bought the contents of his commissary from the estate. Items included glass showcases, bill files, and an iron safe. The safe was used for storing deeds to property, insurance papers and what money was accumulated during the week until it was carried to the bank in town which was done the first of each week.

The houses for the turpentine hands were called "quarters," and constructed close together near the turpentine still for the white hands. About a mile away were the black quarters where the Negroes were housed. None of the houses in either quarter had indoor plumbing. The quarters were heated by fireplaces and cooking was done on wood stoves. A lot of the furniture was home made and corn shucks were used as mattress stuffing. Each house had its own well located in the yard with outhouses, also called privies, out in back.

Asa was ahead of his time with his progressive beliefs about the blacks being educated. Most folks saw no need for their education, and the county did not pay for schools for them, but Asa believed that if they could read and write they would be better employees. (Note: In those days, if you could not write, documents were signed with an "X" and witnessed by those present, and this was a legal signature in the rural South in the early part of the 20th century.) In keeping with this conviction, he constructed a one-room school house in the Negro quarters and hired a teacher to teach them up to the seventh grade. This building also served as a church for them on Sunday when there was usually a black preacher around to conduct services.

In addition to the buildings already described, Asa's growing community also had a grist mill and a sawmill. The sawmill could be a dangerous place; it was powered by a steam engine which pulled the logs into the saw blade. If a log jammed it had to be set free. On one occasion one of the workers jumped on a jammed log to get it realigned correctly with the blade. He fell off the log and before the steam engine could be stopped the blade split him from his buttocks to his waist. Of course he died instantly. It was a very tragic accident, but the life of a country worker could be perilous.

Another building on the property was a two-story building known as the pack house and Lodge Hall. The country Masonic Lodge had needed a new place to meet because the building they had been using was no longer available. Masonic Lodges at that time had to have meeting halls on the 2nd floor. Ground floor lodge halls were not permitted.

The Masons approached Asa, also a Mason, with their problem. He told them he would give them the timber, and they could saw it at his mill and construct the lodge on his property. His only request was that he be given use of the downstairs for storing tobacco until it went to market as well as cotton, and then fertilizer in the spring. Upstairs was kept securely locked since the Masons were a secret organization. The children were told that they kept a mean goat up there and to stay away because it would get them for sure. This Lodge stayed in existence until the 1950s when it consolidated with the Masonic Lodge in town, and this is how the original Harton Lodge came to be re-located upstairs over the pack house on Asa Stall's farm.

These descriptions provide snapshots of the environment in which Asa, Ada and their children, who now numbered 3 since another girl, Inez, had been born in 1920, lived and prospered. The family's home that was described earlier was just about 100 ft. up the road from the commissary, and barns and other out-buildings were all in close proximity. It was a life full of a lot of hard work, and at the same time, it was a life of southern comfort, but changes were coming, and with them, some drama.

SEVEN

Changing Times

By 1915 the automobile began to change things in the rural south, and by the 1920s, the Roaring Twenties, rural society was becoming more mobile and traveling away from their self-contained communities. One of the first automobiles in the Satilla community, as the Harton's area of the county had come to be called, was owned by Jim Harton. He also had a truck. It could haul four barrels of tar although he would allow only three because he worried that it would be overloaded.

In addition to the automobile, World War I also brought change. Many of the boys from the area went away to fight and returned talking about a whole new world of places they had seen. Before then, most folks had not known anybody who had been to such distant lands.

One of Jim Harton's sons, Lott, was not back from the war yet when Mr. Harton died in 1925. The Army was contacted and telegrams sent and received stating that his son was on his way home, and so the family decided to wait for the funeral until he arrived. The undertaker was sent for from town. He came out to the house with the coffin and embalming supplies, and embalmed Jim at home. The fluids were buried in the pecan orchard beside the house.

They laid Mr. Horton out in the coffin in the parlor and waited for Lott. As was the custom, some of the family and friends sat up all night with the body. Well, they scheduled and rescheduled the funeral waiting for him to get home. After a week went by, the body started turning dark and began to smell a little, so the family went ahead and had the funeral without Lott. Wouldn't you know; he arrived the next day. His train from Boston had been delayed in Washington.

After Jim Harton's death, there was talk that he drank himself to death. Even though this was in the noble days of prohibition, alcohol was still available. He would send his black drivers in that car he had bought to Jacksonville, Florida, to bring alcohol back in suitcases. Illegal it may have been but available it certainly was. Doctors had warned Harton that he had to quit drinking or it was going to kill him.

About two weeks after one of these warnings, he called in his driver and said, "Go get me a load of whiskey." The driver tried to beg off going as he had heard what the doctors were telling Mr. Jim.

"Who pays your wages?" Mr. Jim asked him.

The driver said, "You do, Sir."

"Well, then go; it's your job."

In the last years of his life, Jim Harton's business had declined, but there was still a lot of prosperity and some money to be distributed to his heirs upon his death. Ada received two farms and a sum of $8,000 in cash when the estate was settled in 1927. This added to the wealth she and Asa had been amassing. Asa thought they should take the cash and purchase more land. However, Ada put the money in the bank and selected some new furniture for their house.

She went down to Waycross in 1928 and bought a self-player piano, a three-piece parlor suite, a dining room suite consisting of table, eight chairs, buffet and china cabinet, some rugs, and a bedroom set. Asa thought it was a lot of money to spend, but when the bank went bust in 1929, and the rest of the money was gone, Asa said, "Well, at least you got something to show for your money." And, truth was, the new furnishings had improved their house as well as their standing in the community.

Ada made one other purchase, an automobile. She had decided it was time to learn to drive. Everybody thought that she was getting the hang of it until one morning when she decided to go visit her sister over near Sentella Church. She put Elizabeth and Asa Jr. in the car with her and started down the road. Down at the end of the field two hogs came out of the woods and onto the road. Ada forgot she had a horn to blow, so she started hollowing, "Sooie, sooie, pigs," and shoving the pigs with her hand. Well she ran that car right into the ditch. Fortunately nobody was hurt. Asa Jr. walked back to the commissary and got some of the hands with a mule to pull the car out of the ditch. Ada never tried driving again. Asa Jr. was twelve years old at the time, and he could already drive. In those days no driver's license was required. Youngsters who could drive, drove locally whenever they needed to, especially if there was an adult in the car, so naturally Asa Jr. became his ma's chauffeur when she was going anywhere.

All the changes coming to rural Georgia kept Asa Sr. interested in new things and new ways of doing things. He put in an underground gas tank and a gas pump, and the commissary started selling gas. He also constructed a two-car garage to hold the family's cars, and his family became one of the first truly mobile ones in the community in the 1920s.

Another new invention that came to rural life for those of means was electric lighting for their homes. This was accomplished by using a Delco system which was a battery operated plant that generated electricity for lights for Asa's house and the commissary. Large batteries powered a generator which provided much better lighting than kerosene lamps. The Delco system was used until after the coming of REA (Rural Electrification Administration) to the rural south. There were also some appliances, wonders of the day, which could operate off a Delco system. Some of them included an iron, which was a great improvement over irons that had to be heated on the stove, an oscillating fan, and a refrigerator.

All of this prosperity came to a shocking halt in 1929 when the Great Depression gripped the country. Money was scarce, but on the farms of the rural south, of the kind we are recalling here, at least there was enough food from the animals and vegetables grown on the farm. Asa had also saved some money that was not in the bank, and he had money in a bank in Savannah that remained solvent. Therefore, he was able to continue to buy up more land at three-to-five dollars an acre. His holdings doubled during the period of bad economy in the nation, but money was hard to collect, and the accounts owed to the commissary grew. However, if you stayed and worked, Asa saw that you did not go hungry.

So what was a typical work day in this changing environment?

It began when Asa got up at 4 o'clock in the morning. As light began to crack through in the eastern sky, he would go outside and holler real loud. That was the sure alarm clock. He could be heard in both the white and Negro quarters. Everyone was expected to be at work, ready to go by sun-up.

Ada was also up fixing a complete breakfast. The household consisted not only of two adults and their three children, but there were often some live-in cousins or visiting relatives to be fed. The cousins usually worked with Asa Sr. in the business. They also helped with the chores around the farm. Even though Asa Sr. operated a thriving turpentine business and farming operation, he lived on a working farm with milk cows, hogs, chickens, ducks, etc. All of them had to be cared for.

Asa Sr. always headed out immediately after breakfast. He went to the commissary first. It was open every day except Sunday and was attended by his brother-in-law, who was also the bookkeeper.

The early bustle there created lots of noise. Farmers were coming for their mules. Some of them had wagons to load with fertilizer and seed from the pack house. The turpentine wagon rolled by, too, carrying workers to the woods to streak boxes. This wagon picked up first in the white quarters and then the Negro quarters. After every one had left for the day's work, Asa would then go down to the turpentine still and check on things there.

The rest of the day depended on what needed attention. Perhaps fences needed to be mended, or someone might come by wanting to sell a piece of property. This generally required going to look over the land. Asa Sr. was always interested in land, even if it was only twenty acres, and especially if it joined some he already owned. Then a drummer might come by the commissary. If so, Asa Sr. met with him and placed orders for merchandise. His days were always busy.

Over at the house the black help came in at seven. Pearl was the new cook, and now Lucille was doing the cleaning, the washing, and the ironing. Ada supervised the work in the kitchen where a full mid-day meal had to be ready by noon when Asa Sr. came back to eat, along with whomever was at the commissary since they would be invited to dinner. For all the changes happening in the rural south, meals had not changed. They were still breakfast, dinner, and supper with that noon dinner being the large meal of the day, and supper still being little more than leftovers from dinner.

In those days everybody worked so hard physically that the noon meal was an important part of the day. There might be only family at dinner, or there could be as many as ten or twelve others. Even the white workers, or farmers who were working around the place, came to dinner. The black help was fed, too, but still served in the kitchen or on the porch and still had separate dishes, glasses and eating utensils.

When dinner was over and the leftover food put into the food safe and the dishes washed, Ada sat down to sew or went out and worked in her flowers in the yard. Occasionally, she received a visitor from a neighboring farm, perhaps a relative or another farmer's wife. When Asa Sr. came home about dark, supper was warmed and served. When finished, Ada and Asa retired to bed, usually with little conversation.

EIGHT

Lillie

One of Ada's regular visitors was her sister-in-law, Lillie. Lillie was married to Ada's brother, George Harton. Lillie came over to help sew and make new dresses. She was quite talented and could cut out dresses just from looking at pictures in catalogs and magazines. She could also design and make curtains, draperies, and slip covers. These were all natural talents she had honed with practice.

Sometimes Lillie would stop by the commissary to pick up supplies for her household. If Asa Sr. was in, they would strike up a conversation; there was just a natural attraction between the two of them. They were able to talk easily and freely without much effort. Asa Sr. also, on occasion, stopped by her house for a glass of tea in the afternoon when he was out driving around to his farms. It seemed all quite innocent since they were in-laws, but after a time they both realized there was a great attraction developing between them. Even so, since they were both married and had children, they both felt there could be no disruption of the family ties. In spite of this acknowledgement, Asa Sr. began to stop by more frequently, and Lillie was often present with her children at his house helping Ada make new slipcovers for the parlor, so that they saw more and more of one another.

One Sunday, Ada's sister, Lottie, came home from church with

Ada for Sunday dinner and was staying over until Monday. Her husband had gone to Waycross on business so she was out visiting. After dinner, they were sitting on the front porch rocking. In the course of the conversation Lottie asked, "Why is Asa over at George's and Lillie's so many afternoons? I don't think George is home, and I'm told Asa was there two afternoons last week."

You could have knocked Ada over with a feather. She stopped rocking and after a minute asked, "Are you sure your information is right?"

Lottie said, "Well, I've seen his car there myself, but I didn't think anything about it until Sara Ann Quinn mentioned it to me. Oh, Lord, Ada I should've kept my mouth shut. Lillie is here a lot and you two are like sisters."

Ada said, "Well, yes, but I had no idea about this."

"Well, Ada, just ask Asa about it, and I'm sure he'll have a good explanation. He is devoted to you."

Ada thought for a little bit. Dead silence filled the air. She was thinking to herself what she would do. She decided for the moment to say nothing and told Lottie not to mention it to anyone because she wasn't going to let on that she had heard such a rumor. After all, it was probably nothing to be concerned about.

Lillie went over to Ada's the next week, and they finished those slip covers for the parlor. Nothing was said, and they got on fine. When Lillie started to leave for the day, she said, "See you in a week or two, and we can do new draperies for your bedroom if you get the fabric for them."

Ada decided she would just approach the subject and see what happened. "Lillie, has Asa been stopping by your house lately in the afternoon?"

Lillie was quite stunned, but she calmly replied, "Well, yes, he has stopped by a time or two for a glass of tea. I do enjoy talking with him."

"I see," Ada said flatly. "Well, I'm not sure it is such a good idea. I have heard some talk, and I don't like gossip, and I am sure you don't either."

"Well, I had no idea, but people will talk if they get a chance. He has stopped by for a glass of tea occasionally, but it never crossed my mind that people would talk or think anything about my brother-in-law paying a visit."

On that note she left to go home.

Ada went on into the kitchen to get supper ready and forgot about the conversation. She had three children to be concerned with. Elizabeth, the oldest, was sixteen now, Asa Jr. was 12, and Inez was six. Elizabeth had finished seventh grade and was still at home, so she was expected to help around the house. One evening while she was helping Ada get supper ready, they were talking about the church social Elizabeth was invited to Saturday night. Will Bryant had asked her to go. He was 18 and lived over at Uncle Avery's place. She had been seeing him occasionally for about three or four months.

Ada said, "We will have to get that pretty blue flowered dress ready for you to wear, but you must ask your pa if you can go when he comes home to supper."

When Asa came in, he washed up and as soon as they were at the table, Elizabeth said, "Pa, can I go to the social Saturday night with Will?"

"You sure are seeing a lot of him lately," Asa said. "Ya gettin' sweet on him?"

Elizabeth blushed and said, "I don't know. He's nice."

Asa Jr. piped up, "Elizabeth's got a beau. When are ya gettin' married?"

"No time soon! Don't even think of it," Ada exclaimed.

After supper Ada sat on the swing, and Asa came out and took a seat. Ada said,

"I've had some news that bothers me." She stopped.

"Well, what is it that's bothering you?" Asa asked.

"Well, it's been brought to my attention that you have been seen a lot lately in the afternoon stopping by Lillie's and George's – when George isn't home. It's causing a lot of gossip."

Asa said, "Well, Ada, I just stop by for a glass of tea once in a while. Lillie is interesting to talk to."

"I think if you want to talk to a woman you better come by here," Ada replied coolly, "and I will fix you some iced tea, and we will talk. You know how rumors get started."

Asa changed the subject and started talking about the crops and when they would be ready for market and how much tar was bringing a barrel.

Nothing more was said about Lillie, and Ada and Asa went to bed as if nothing had been.

NINE

Big News

About three weeks passed after Elizabeth went to the church social with Will. He had been by every Sunday since to see her, and she had slipped off to the fish pond to see him once or twice during the week.

Tuesday morning she got up and didn't feel well. She told Ada she was sick. Ada looked at her and said, "Breakfast will make you feel better."

Elizabeth ate a few bites and suddenly ran out to the porch and lost it all. Ada suggested she go and lie back down. By dinner she felt some better, but the next two mornings were the same.

The third morning Asa Sr. had already left for work, but was still down at the commissary. Ada sent Pearl over to ask Asa to come back by the house when he left on his rounds. Pearl went down to the commissary where Asa was seated on a bench. She said, "Mr. Asa, Miss Ada say she need you to come by the house when you leaves the commissary."

"All right, Pearl, tell her I will."

He took his time and stopped by about 9:30. He found Ada and Pearl on the back porch shelling peas for dinner. "Pearl said you wanted me."

Ada said, "Yes, come out front with me."

They walked through the hall to the front porch, and Ada said, "Elizabeth is sick. This makes three mornings in a row. I fear she's pregnant."

"What the hell are you thinking woman?" Asa nearly shouted.

"I am just telling you I think her and Will, well... you know."

"Have you asked her?"

"No; I wanted to talk to you first. Should I take her to Dr. Hall in town or what?"

"Yes, unless she admits to you that she and Will have been fooling around. Go ask her now, and see what she has to say. I'll wait here."

Ada went inside. Elizabeth was lying down. "How do you feel?"

"Just awful, Mama. I'm just as sick as I can be."

"Elizabeth, have you and Will been fooling around?"

"What do you mean, Mama?" Elizabeth responded, trying to look naïve.

"You know exactly what I mean!"

"Oh! No, Mama. You know I wouldn't do that."

"Well," Ada said, "then we better go see Dr. Hall. It might be your appendix. Better yet, since you're so sick, I'll just have him come out. He may have to operate on you."

Ada got up to go out, and Elizabeth realized this was serious. She rose up on the bed and said, "Wait, Mama. I lied. Will and I have been messin' around. You don't think I am gonna have a baby?" she asked with eyes opened wide.

"Well Elizabeth, that's what usually happens," was the exasperated reply. "You ought to know better! I could just skin you alive!"

"Don't tell Pa, he will kill me!"

"What do you expect me to do? You can't be sick without a reason or have a baby without him knowing. He is waiting for me out front now. I've got to go talk to him."

"Oh my, oh my" Elizabeth fretted. "What am I gonna do?"

Ada found Asa pacing the front yard. He looked up. "What is it?"

"She and Will…I'm pretty sure she's pregnant. I'll send for Dr. Hall."

"Well if that's the case, she and Will will have to get married and the sooner the better! I should beat the hell out of Will, but what's done is done. Don't bother having Dr. Hall come out. I'm sure you know what's wrong with her. I'll find Will and have a serious, man to man, talk with him as soon as I can."

Asa headed off to check on the turpentine hands. He did not come home at dinner time, which was unusual. Ada wondered why he didn't show up but figured he was busy or perhaps he had driven into town, although he usually told her if he had to go to town.

She would not find out the truth about where he was until several weeks later, but he went over to Lillie's. He had dinner with her and George, and when George went back to work, he told Lillie about Elizabeth. Lillie was very sympathetic to Asa, but made the comment that Ada should have instructed her better. Then she went over and put her arms around him, and gave him a big hug, and softly drawled, "You deserve so much better than all this, you dear, sweet man."

Asa just loved every minute of this attention. He certainly was not used to it at home. The energy of the moment took over, and suddenly, they were in an embrace. Then Asa kissed Lillie full in the mouth. She almost fainted, and Asa was completely stunned by the way he felt. He had never had feelings like those for Ada.

After a moment they both recovered. Asa looked at Lillie and said, "You mean a lot to me, and I really like being with you I think much more than with anyone else."

Lillie said, "Asa I love you – everything about you. What are we to do? I guess we mustn't see each other alone any more. This would just be a terrible scandal that would wreck the whole family."

"I'm sure you're right, but how can we not see each other? I believe we belong together, that we make each other happy."

With no resolution and flustered about the state they found themselves in, in-laws in love, they parted for the afternoon.

TEN
Ruined

Asa Sr. left Lillie with a happy, yet heavy heart, and more than just a little bit of guilt. He wondered what he should do. Well, first things first. He had to find Will Bryant and talk to him!

When he rounded the curve at the Avery Farm, he saw Will plowing in the corn field. He pulled up to the side of the road and walked over to the fence. He waited for Will to come to the end of the row. When Will saw him, he stopped to speak. "How you doing, Mr. Asa?" Will hollered.

Frowning, Asa hollered back, "Come here young man, I got a matter to take up with you." Will ambled over, and Asa just blurted it out. "It seems you and Elizabeth been fooling around, and she got herself pregnant. Now you listen to me, Will Bryant, I expect you to do the right thing by her! You will marry her and right away!"

"Mr. Asa there ain't no problem with that. I really do like her a lot. Can I…well… come by this evening and set things right?"

Will seemed calm and agreeable, so all Asa could say was, "That'll be fine. You come to supper, and we will make all the arrangements."

When Asa got home, he told Ada that Will was coming to supper and things would be arranged for him and Elizabeth to get married right away. Ada then told Elizabeth that Will was coming to supper and that her pa said arrangements would be made. Elizabeth was not quite sure what that meant, but Pa was not in a mood to be questioned. He seemed to be in a deep study about something. No doubt it was Lillie as much as it was Elizabeth and Will troubling him.

As he said he would, Will arrived about 6:30. Elizabeth went out on the porch to see him. She thought he looked quite handsome, but that he seemed terribly uneasy. "Mama said you were coming to supper but why tonight? Is everything okay?" Elizabeth asked.

"Well, I come to ask you to marry me. Your pa told me you was in a family way."

"Oh, Will, yes, I will marry you if Pa says it's okay. That would make me very happy."

"He already said it was fine 'cause we got to do the right thing."

Everyone came into supper and sat down. Nobody said a word until Asa broke the silence. "You may as well all know; Will and Elizabeth are getting married Saturday. Ada you can make the arrangements to have old Judge Camp come out to do the honors."

"That is short notice," Ada replied.

"Well, short notice or not that's the way it's gonna be. You get Pearl busy with the cooking and let the family know so they'll come if they can. I'd say 5:00 o'clock with eatin' afterwards."

When supper was over, Asa ordered, "Will come out here with me." They walked off toward the boiler shed. "Will, you be good to Elizabeth, and she'll make you a good wife. I'll arrange a house for you soon. Do you intend to continue to work for Avery or should I find you a job?"

"Well, Mr. Asa, Cousin Ronnie got a job down in Waycross at the railroad shop. It pays pretty good. I was thinking we might just move down there and make a start for ourselves, but we would need a car so as we could come back up here for visiting."

"If that's what you want, I will arrange a car instead of a house for you. Elizabeth has a little money which I will give to her to help you get started."

Meantime, the minute supper was over, Ada and Elizabeth had begun to make plans for the wedding. "You can wear that cream colored dotted Swiss dress Lillie made for you, and I'll arrange the meal with Pearl in the morning. Now you be good to Will after you're married. It'll all be okay now." Ada's mind was easing about Elizabeth's situation.

When Saturday arrived, the house was all abuzz with the fixings for the wedding. About four o'clock folks started arriving, including Lillie and George and their children. The formalities did not take long, and by five thirty everybody was already eating and having a good time.

Lillie had not seen Asa since that afternoon embrace and kiss. For today she had told herself that she would just try to avoid interacting with him if she could. Things went as planned until she was helping Ada clean up in the kitchen. That's when Ada asked, "Lillie, would you take this buttermilk out to the ice house for me?"

Lillie did, but as she rounded the corner, there was Asa, and they more or less stumbled into one another. Asa grabbed her to steady her on her feet, letting his arms go around her. Just as he did Ada came around the corner to get ice for the lemonade that they were going to serve with the cake and home made ice cream.

Ada gasped, "Well, I never! All the gossip is true then! You two are sweet on each other. Lillie, you hussy, and you my own sister-in-law and over here all the time helping me sew and being so nice!"

Ada turned quickly and hurried back to the house. She was all in tears, but she dried them in the kitchen, and as far as everyone else knew it was a perfect wedding party. However, the damage was done. There would be a high price to pay over the discovery of Asa and Lillie in each other's arms.

ELEVEN

Everything Boils Over

Sunday morning the whole family sat down for breakfast, including Will and Elizabeth. They had been given the guest bedroom for their first night of marriage, and so they were still home with the rest of the family. Ada was very quiet at the table. Asa Sr. acted as if everything was fine, but if you knew them well you would have known that things were not like they ought to be.

Asa Sr. said, "I'm going into town tomorrow to see about some transportation for the two of you, Elizabeth. Will tells me he wants to take a job in Waycross at the train yards if his cousin can get him on, so you two will need a way to come and go and come back to visit me and your ma."

Ada glared at Asa and just said, "Oh!" and nothing else.

Asa continued to act as if everything was fine. He asked Ada if she was going to church down at Zora.

"No indeed. The Lord has given me enough to bear today, and I have a terrible headache. Asa Jr. can drive Elizabeth and Will and Inez to church. I think I had best lie down." With that she immediately got up from the table and went to her room.

Inez said, "What ails Ma? She ain't never feeling bad."

"Well, it's just all this weddin' and Elizabeth moving away; it's just been a lot for her happenin' so sudden and all," Asa replied.

The girls cleaned up with Pearl's help and put up the dishes. Then Pearl said, "Girls you better go check on your ma and then get ready for church. I'll get dinner ready before I leave and put it in the warming oven. Don't bring nobody home from church with you today cause you know Miss Ada don't feel good."

After everybody left for church, Asa went down to the still and walked over to the pond. He picked up one of the fishing poles they kept there and cast the line. It wasn't too long before Uncle John, his bookkeeper, came walking along and stopped to chat.

Asa Sr. asked, "What do ya know today? Everybody seemed to enjoy the weddin' doin's yesterday."

"Shore did," John responded, "but the women folk was a buzzin' accordin' to my wife about you havin' an affair with Lillie."

"Hell, John, you don't believe that do you?"

"Well now; I don't know. Shore is an awful lot of smoke to be no fire."

"Well, John, you are my best friend and my brother-in-law, so I'll just tell you. There is some fire there. It happened before I knew it. It wasn't planned. It just happened. We enjoyed each other's company, and it just happened."

"What ya gonna do, Asa?"

"Nothin'. I care a great deal for Ada and the children. Nothin' can come of it. It just has to be over as if it never was."

"What does Ada have to say?"

"Well, she ain't said nothin'. She saw me catch Lillie in my arms to keep her from fallin' yesterday, and she ran hot for a minute, but I ain't said nothin' to her about it. I really was just stoppin' Lillie from fallin'. Anyway Ada went back to bed with a headache this morning, and we ain't talked at all."

"Well, you better talk to her. It ain't like Ada to go back to bed for no reason. You better talk to her real soon!"

"Lordy, I don't need these kinda problems. Guess I should've seen 'em coming though."

"Well you think about how to get it all squared away, and I'll see you at the commissary in the mornin'."

Asa lay on the pond bank thinking about all the mess he was in. He took out his pocket watch to see what time it was. It was noon so he walked back to the house.

When the children got back from church at twelve thirty, Elizabeth went in and checked on her mama. "We're back. You ready to eat, Mama?"

"Don't feel like it. You put out what Pearl left in the warmer, and y' all go ahead and eat. Just bring me a glass of ice tea and get me an aspirin to take."

Conversation was lively at the dinner table with all the talk about Elizabeth and Will moving to Waycross, and who was at church and what they had on. Inez piped up. "Pa, next time that drummer comes from Savannah I want you to order me a big straw hat with flowers. Minnie Johnson had on one her pa got 'er last month when supplies came up to 'em."

Asa said, "I'll see. You don't need no fancy hat though. You're pretty as a picture without one."

When dinner was finished, Elizabeth and Inez cleared the table. Asa Sr., Will, and Asa Jr., went out on the porch.

Asa Sr. asked, "When do ya think you'll be movin' to Waycross, Will?"

"Well, Sir, I need to go down and make sure I can get on at the train yard, and I need to tell Mr. Avery I'm quitting if I can get on. I'll need to find me and Elizabeth a place to live. My cousin said I could stay with them if I came, but they don't know about Elizabeth and me yet."

Asa Jr. spoke up. "I'm gonna go change my clothes and go fishin'," and he left the older men to talk.

Pretty soon Elizabeth came out on the porch. "Will, let's go for a walk, and Inez wants to tag along." They walked off down toward the creek leaving Asa Sr. on the porch by himself.

He thought a little bit and then decided he should go check on Ada and just face the music. He quietly knocked on the door and entered her room. Ada was sitting up in a rocking chair.

"You feeling better, Dear?" he asked trying to sound encouraging. He may as well have spit in her face.

"You bastard! Why are you in here? Shouldn't you be off to meet Lillie somewhere? How could you and with my sister-in-law?"

"Ada, please… now calm down. It's all a mistake. You mean everything to me. You know that. This thing with Lillie is all blown up. You know I want only you."

"It's too late for that now. You've made me the laughin' stock of the whole district. How can I ever show my face at church again, or anywhere else? Just get out!! Get your things and go!! I don't want to see you. We're finished."

Asa never expected this. *Damn*, he thought. *Her temper was as bad as her father's, when she got riled up*. Not knowing what else to do, he turned and quietly walked out of the room.

Just as he got to the front door, George Harton was getting off his horse. You could tell he had ridden hard. "Evenin', George."

"Evenin', hell! You son of a bitch! I oughta get my shot gun and blow a hole in your ass. I'll have your hide for this. Lillie has owned up to it all. She's in love with you, you asshole, stoppin' by when I'm at work!"

"Now hold on, George. You got this all wrong. I ain't in love with Lillie. You need to go home and work things out with your wife. I just talked to Ada and she understands it just ain't like it looks."

That's when Ada came out the front door. "Understand!" "George dear," and she began to cry. "We are ruined, ruined." She composed herself and stopped crying. Then she bitterly announced. "I want Asa to just go. This is just too awful. George you go on home now. They ain't worth you killing either of 'em." She went back inside.

Jarred by all of this, Asa Sr. finally realized there was way more of a problem than he had bargained for. George got on his horse and left, still mad as hell.

Asa Sr. thought to himself that maybe this would blow over, but it sure did not feel like it would. He wondered if he could change Ada's mind, wondered if he could get Lillie and George back together. He decided he would go into town and spend the night at the Duncan House and tend to his business on Monday morning and get that car for Elizabeth and Will. He went in and told Ada he was going into town to spend the night so he could get an early start in the morning.

Her cold reply was, "Go and stay and take Lillie with you."

He got in his car and drove off thinking that surely things will look better when he came back tomorrow.

TWELVE
Big Changes

By the time Asa Sr. finished getting a used Model T Ford for Elizabeth and Will and going to the bank, it was dinner time, so he stopped back in at the Duncan House to eat. When he arrived at the farm it was mid-afternoon, and he went straight to the commissary to check on things.

As he walked in, John said, "Asa, where were ya this morning? George Harton has been over here raising hell. Lillie left him this morning, took George's car, and she and the kids went to her family. He's been here and up to the house to see Ada. He's sayin' he's gonna sue ya for everything ya got. Ada sent Asa Jr. down here with a message for ya to come by the house as soon as ya got back."

Wearily, Asa asked, "Is there anything else I need to know before I go try and talk to Ada?"

"No, everything else is goin' good today. We're gettin' low on flour, but it's due here by Thursday which will be in time to fill Saturday's grocery orders."

Asa went on up to the house. Ada had been watching for him and met him on the porch. "It's all out in the open. Lillie has left George and says she is going to marry you," she announced flatly.

"First I heard about this marriage business. I'm married to you."

"Not for long! I have packed all your clothes in those two trunks. Take them and go. We are through!" she emphasized with a raised voice.

"Ada, don't you think this is a little hasty? Can't we talk about this and work somethin' out?"

"Certainly not; you made your choice. Now go! I do expect you to look after the children's needs and mine, however, so you decide how after you think it over."

"Ada this is not what I want."

"Well, you should've thought of that before you started stoppin' at Lillie's for iced tea and got this mess brewed up. Asa I cannot and will not stay with you after all that has happened. It would be bad enough if it wasn't so close in the family, but this… this is unforgivable."

Asa Sr. went back down to the commissary and told John that he guessed it was over for him and Ada because she was determined she had had enough. John said, "You can stay with us for awhile until ya decide what ya wanna do."

"I'll go back into town to the Duncan House tonight. I'll be back out here first thing in the morning. I need to see Judge Hall before I come back out and see what he has to say about a divorce. May as well get it over with if this is the way it has to be."

As he started out to the car, the sheriff came up the steps. "How ya doing, Asa? I got some papers here for ya. Bad news I'm sure."

Asa was surprised, but he took the papers and signed for them. Then he went back in and tossed the papers at John. "What the hell is this?"

John opened the papers and read them. "Well, Asa, it's like this. George Harton is suing ya for alienation of affection where his wife, Lillie, is concerned. He claims ya owe him $20,000 for the pain and suffering you've brought on him."

Asa asked, "Can he do that?"

"Well, I guess he can. Seems he has. I ain't never heard of it bein'

BIG CHANGES | 55

done in this county, but over in Emanuel County it was done some years ago, and the man had to pay some money for breakin' up a marriage, but never heard of it bein' done in these parts."

"Reckon I'll be in town a little longer in the morning. Better see Lester Moore, my attorney, as well as the judge."

With that said, Asa Sr. had one of the hands unload the trunks from his car and stash them behind the counter; then he headed off toward town. When he got to the road that turned off to Satilla Church, he decided he would go by the Harper place and see if Lillie was there with her folks. Yep, sure enough she was there. Mrs. Harper came to the door and gave Asa a warm greeting.

"Could I see Lillie?"

"Well, of course, come on in the front room here, and I'll get her. She's in my sewing room making me some new kitchen curtains."

Asa Sr. had a seat and waited. He thought she seemed friendly enough. Then he thought more about it. *Why shouldn't she be? If Lillie and me get together, they'll be better off. After all, it is local knowledge that I'm well off.*

About a minute passed before Lillie sailed in with a glass of iced tea. She was all smiles. "Asa, I'm so glad you came by. I've been worried sick about you and so afraid you would be mad with me," she cooed. Then she bent down and planted a big kiss on his cheek.

"I ain't mad with you, but things sure are in a mess since you moved out on George. He's suing me for alienation of affection claimin' I broke up his happy home."

"Oh, Asa, I hate that this has happened, but I can't help the fact that I love you, and I miss you something awful when I don't see you. I know I can make you happy and even though there's a lot of trouble now, I'll make it up to you."

"Now, Lillie, hold on just a minute. Ada has kicked me out and is mad at both of us, and we're both still married. I think we shouldn't see each other for a time until we are both free. Then we can see how we feel about the future."

"I didn't mean to hurt Ada or George, but I can't help how I feel about you."

"Well we have a mess to deal with. I'm on my way to town. I'll meet with the judge and my lawyer in the morning."

"Oh, Asa, do you have to go? Can't you stay to supper?"

"No I don't think so. I best be on my way before somebody sees my car out front which would just be more fuel for the gossip that's already rampant."

Asa got up out of the chair, and Lillie put her arms around him. His automatically went around her. It just felt like the natural thing to do, like it was supposed to be that they belonged together. He held her for what seemed like a long time looking down at her, and then he gave her a long, passionate kiss.

"I must go now. We'll just have to see how it all works out." He drove on into town. *I believe she could make me happy. She's nothing like Ada. Ada has never been so warm and affectionate.*

Asa spent another night at the Duncan House and early next morning went to see Lester Moore, his attorney. After telling Lester all of his problems, he asked him how much trouble it would be and how long it would take to get a divorce from Ada.

"It will take several months here, but if you want one in a hurry go out to Arkansas. You can get one there in a matter of weeks. I can give you the name of an attorney to see in Hot Springs." Lester smiled. "You can relax at the springs while you get a divorce."

"Give me his name. I think that's what I'll do – go away, get a divorce, let things cool off a bit."

Then Lester added, "You have time. The suit George has against you won't come up for at least three months; that's the next court session."

"Lester, does George have a chance with this lawsuit against me?"

"Can't say for sure, but if you aren't seeing Lillie after your divorce and the case does come up, he probably won't stand much of a chance. Have you two been seen together?"

"Well, no, but it has been said that my car was there at her and George's in the afternoon while George was away, and I can't deny that. But there has been no relations between us, you understand."

"Okay, we'll just have to see, but these kinds of cases seldom go very far."

"Well, I'm going back out to the farm and talk to John about lookin' after the business and to Asa Jr., too. He's only fourteen, but he can take care of some things while I'm away."

Asa Sr. left the lawyer's office and went straight to the train station. Phillip Hughes was in charge of things at the depot. "Mornin', Asa. You expectin' a shipment from Savannah?"

"No, Phillip. I need a ticket to Hot Springs, Arkansas."

"What you goin' there for, to get the cure?"

"No, just got some business to tend to."

"Well, let's see. Your best bet is to go from here to Macon, over to Montgomery, then to Jackson, and up to Little Rock. From there you can go on to Hot Springs."

"Sounds fine to me. Fix me up."

With his ticket bought, Asa Sr. got in his car. He would be leaving at noon tomorrow, so he went straight to the commissary and told John what he had decided to do.

"Willis, go get Asa Jr. He's probably in the corn crib doing chores."

Willis went off toward the house to find Asa Jr. In a little bit they both came back to the store.

Asa explained to his son that he was going to Arkansas to get a divorce from his ma because of all the hell she had raised about Lillie. Asa Jr. was upset, but felt a little proud that his pa was telling him all this stuff and trusted him to help look after the farm while he was away. He asked his pa, "How long will ya be gone?"

"Maybe a month. Now you're to mind your ma and look after your little sister and check in with John. You're the man of the house now. I want ya to drive me back into town to the Duncan House, and then ya take good care of my car while I'm gone."

Asa Jr. felt ten feet tall with Pa treating him so grown up.

"I will write to ya when I get to Hot Springs, and to John."

John told Asa Sr., "We'll do the best we can while you're gone."

"I know ya will. Let Asa Jr. help as much as he can. I'll fix it at the bank in the morning before I leave. If ya need money before I get back they'll have it for ya, or ya can draw a draft on Carson Company in Savannah from the tar account."

Asa Sr. and Asa Jr. headed to town. Not much was said on the way until finally Asa Jr. asked, "Pa, are you and Ma really splittin' up? Where are we gonna live?"

"I'm afraid so, but y'all will stay right where you're at," replied Asa. "I'll still be around, but this is what your ma wants 'cause she's just sure I've been having an affair with your Aunt Lillie even though it ain't true."

Asa Jr. put his pa out at the Duncan House and started for home. He had an awful lot to think about and to brag about to Ma and his sister. Pa left him in charge!

THIRTEEN
Divorce

Asa Jr. got back home about six o'clock, parked the car in the garage, and walked across the road to the house. Ada was on the porch and watched him drive up. Her first question was, "What are you doin' in your pa's car?"

Asa Jr. began to tell her all about what had been said and where Pa was going. Ada teared up and softly said, "Well, I guess he's got it the way he wanted it."

"Ma, don't cry. Everything'll be fine. I'll look after everything for ya."

Asa Jr. left his ma on the porch and went to take care of his chores. He had lots to do including feeding the cows, chickens and hogs and then check to see if all the mules were in the barn and fed. When he was finished, he went back to the house for supper. Nobody said much, and everybody went on to bed early.

The next morning things went on as normally as they could without Asa Sr. there. Asa Jr. and Inez headed off to school even though Asa Jr. tried to talk Ma out of making him go by reminding her that Pa wanted him to look after things while he was gone. Ada told him, "John will take care of things just fine. Now you scoot on off to school. You still got learnin' to do."

About eleven o'clock, while Ada and Pearl were fixing dinner, Lottie rolled up. You could tell just from the sight of her that she had plenty on her mind. Ada told Pearl to set another plate and to send Elizabeth to the commissary to ask John how many would be coming up to eat. Lottie hit the bottom step hollering for Ada.

"Here I am, Lottie, what's all the excitement about?"

"Are you okay? I just heard last night at the prayer meetin' over at the Quinn's that Lillie left George and George is suing Asa and Asa's left town!" She was breathless with it all! "What are you gonna do?"

"Well, Lottie, not much I can do the way I see it. Yes, Asa has moved out of here. I told him to. And now he's gone over to Hot Springs to get a divorce. There's nothin' to do."

"Nothin'! Ada are you just outa your mind?" Lottie's voice was getting shrill and loud. "You need to be gettin' yourself a lawyer. If he gets a divorce and marries that hussy, what do you intend to live on? And what about the children? You know she's got two already, and if they get married, they may have more. You need more than the two farms our pa left you, and who's goin' to look after them for you? Lord, Ada, you need help! You gotta do somethin' to protect your children and your home here! Or do you want to have to move and just let her take over here?"

All this was too much for Ada, and she began to cry. "Oh, Ada, I didn't mean to upset you so, but somebody's gotta wake you up!"

"You don't think Asa would try to move me out, do you?"

"Well, I don't know. Who would have thought he would take up with Lillie, her being such a good friend to you and in the family and all that?"

"I guess I had better give this some thought. Who will I get? I don't know any lawyers."

"Well, if I were you, I'd go down to Baxley and get Jeff Upshaw. He's supposed to be very good, and he won't be in cahoots with the ones in Hazlehurst like Judge Hall would be seeing he's from here. Do you want me to go with you, Ada?"

DIVORCE | 61

"No, I will get Asa Jr. to drive me down there in the morning and try to see him."

The group sat down for dinner. After they finished eating, Lottie took her leave. After her previous ruckus, all she said was, "I'll see you in a day or two." She left thinking to herself that she surely had done her good deed for the week.

In the quiet house Ada continued to ruminate over her situation. She decided she probably had better go see about getting a lawyer. *Lottie may be right. She is pretty smart. She's run that farm since her husband died five years ago.*

Ada didn't mention what she was doing until the next morning while they were at breakfast. She informed Asa Jr. that he would be staying home from school that day because she needed him to drive her down to Baxley on business.

Inez piped up "Ma, can't I go too?"

"No you can't. You aren't needed, and Asa Jr. is 'cause he's got to drive. Anyway, you can't afford to miss school. Your last grades weren't that good."

Ada got Inez off to school and Pearl settled into her chores. "We'll be back by mid-afternoon if not sooner," she told Pearl. "If anybody asks where I am, just say I've gone off with Asa Jr. on business."

The twelve mile drive took about an hour. Hard rains the week before had left the road in rough shape. When they got to Baxley, Ada said, "Stop at the post office and ask where to find the law office of Jeff Upshaw."

Asa Jr. did as he was told and got the directions. It turned out that Upshaw's office was actually right next to the post office over the dry goods store. Ada and Asa Jr. made their way upstairs where Ada asked the clerk if she might see Mr. Jeff Upshaw.

He replied, "Just a minute, Ma'am. Who should I say wants to see him?"

"Mrs. Ada Harton Stall."

Mr. Upshaw came right out. "Morning, Ma'am. Please, come right in." Right in Ada went but not before instructing Asa Jr. to wait where he was.

When he had closed the door, Upshaw said, "Are you Jim Harton's daughter?"

"Yes," Ada softly answered.

"I was a great admirer of you father and handled a number of things for him. It would be a pleasure to assist you if I can."

Ada related all of the marital problems saying that she supposed she needed to protect herself, or at least her children's interests, now that Asa had gone to Hot Springs to get a divorce.

"Well, I am somewhat familiar with what Asa has. Now there is a question as to whether this divorce will be recognized in Georgia unless you agree to it, so here's what I suggest. We need to take action, like a court injunction, to keep him from disposing of anything until he has settled with you, and you have agreed to the divorce."

Ada said, "I already agreed to the divorce. I'm so hurt by this whole affair. I just want him to go away."

"But my dear, you have not legally agreed to anything. Now what would you like to obtain for you and your three children?"

"Well, I already have two farms, so what I would like from him is a farm with a home place for each of the children and for my farms to be managed for me, as well as his children's farms until they are old enough and can handle things themselves."

"Sounds very reasonable to me, especially since there seems to be a possible charge of adultery against him; that case is strengthened by George Harton's suit for alienation of affection. Of course, we will also require Mr. Stall to pay my fees as a condition of settlement. I will need you to come back down next Monday to sign some papers. About the same time as you got here this morning will be fine."

Ada decided she would not say anything to anyone, not even the children, about what she was doing. So when she and Asa Jr. drove home, she let on to him she was just doing her will.

"Ah, Ma, you ain't sick, are ya?" He was concerned.

"No, no" she replied quickly. "Just takin' care of business."

Things with Asa Sr.'s family went on as if all were normal. Then on Monday, Ada kept Asa Jr. home from school again. They drove back to Upshaw's office, and she signed the papers.

Upshaw told Ada, "These will be waiting on Asa when he gets back. If he's smart, he will agree to all this without a fight. Otherwise, his property will be tied up, and this will go to court. Besides, he probably won't have a valid divorce, so this should take care of that problem."

"I hope so. I don't want to take him to court or try to prove that he and Lillie committed adultery. There is enough talk and embarrassment already for all of us in the family."

"Hold your head high, Mrs. Stall. You have nothing to hide or be ashamed of. You have the reputation of a good wife and mother. Mr. Stall is the one now with a tarnished reputation."

FOURTEEN
Adjusting

Life moved on but just did not seem the same without Asa Sr. at home. Ada continued her daily routine of having dinner ready for as many as John brought to the house from the commissary. Inez and Asa Jr. continued to go to school while he took charge of as much as he could for his ma. He also checked in regularly with Uncle John who had received one letter from Asa Sr.. Asa Jr. also received a letter from his pa, again instructing him to take care of as much as he could until he got back, and so after about a month things settled into the usual run of the mill pattern. It was already late August, and the cotton would soon be ready to pick as well as the corn. Fodder would also have to be pulled for feed for the horses, cows, chickens, and hogs for the upcoming winter.

The first week in September Asa Sr. arrived back in Hazlehurst from Hot Springs and went directly to Lester Moore's office. He gave Lester a copy of the divorce papers from Arkansas.

Lester looked them over and said, "Well they ain't entirely legal in Georgia unless Ada will agree to the divorce."

Asa replied, "Well she said that's what she wanted so I'm sure she will."

"Don't be so sure. I saw Jeff Upshaw at District Court in Brunswick, and he said he has some papers for you and for me to let him know when you're back in town. I believe Ada has got him as her lawyer, so it may not be as easy as you think to get her to agree to this."

Asa said, "Oh hell, I can see her family has done gone and got involved. You got time to drive me down to Upshaw's and let's see what he's got? The sooner this is over, the better. I got to get on with the business of making money. I need to tend to gettin' the crops gathered in and running the turpentine business."

"Well, yes I can go with you down there to Upshaw's this afternoon, and we'll see what we can do."

The men went to dinner at the Duncan House and left for Baxley directly afterwards, arriving about two thirty in the afternoon. They went to Upshaw's office, but he wasn't there. He had gone over to the courthouse. His clerk said that he would go and tell him they were there. In a few minutes, Jeff Upshaw came in.

"Gentlemen, to what do I owe the honor of this visit?"

Lester said "Well you indicated you had some papers for my client when he got back in town. He got back on the early train this morning, came to my office, and here we are."

"Well, Asa, you're looking fine. Hot Springs must have been good for you," drawled Upshaw.

Asa dryly replied, "Not really under the circumstances."

"Well yes, I do understand you have a few women problems these days, so we may as well get right to it. Come on into my office."

"Asa, your wife came down to see me and told me the two of you had separated and that you went on over to Hot Springs to get a divorce. I explained to her she would have to sign papers agreeing to this for it to be legal in Georgia. She said she would agree, but there're a few things she wants."

"First she wants each of the children of your marriage to have a farm with at least seventy-five acres and a house equal to that of the present residence. She has signed papers that, if filed with the Court, will prevent you from doing any business without her approval until this is settled. She does not wish to bring charges of adultery against you unless necessary because she wants no further scandal. The second thing she wants is for you to look after her property, and the children's until they are able to look after it themselves, and to make sure she and the children are paid all their profits for the rest of her life."

"I have not filed this with the court yet. You can consider that this is your notice as it would be served to you by the sheriff and the court, if we can settle this without going to court. Now, Asa, I'm not your attorney, but you already have a lawsuit against you by George Harton for breaking up his marriage. George and Lillie are already divorced. I'm sure Lester will tell you that this strengthens George's case. Gentlemen, why don't you use my other office so you can look over these papers? Maybe we can settle this in a friendly manner."

Lester and Asa Sr. took the papers and went to the other office. Asa said, "I be damn Lester; this action by Ada is quite a surprise. I can see George and Lottie in this or she wouldn't have done such a thing."

Lester replied, "Well she is within her rights and she isn't trying to take everything you got and close you down. In my opinion, if she goes to court, she could get this and more. The court will have sympathy for a woman in her situation, innocent and disgraced and all. You know that."

Asa said, "Well I reckon that's right. What she wants ain't too bad; after all it's for the children as much or more than for her, and they are mine. Okay, Lester, let's just tell Upshaw we will probably agree to what she wants, but that we'll get back to him in a day or two."

So that is what Lester did. "We will be back soon, a day or two after we see which farms we can transfer."

When they got back in the car, Asa Sr. said, "Lester, how 'bout taking me out to the farm and stop by the Commissary so I can get my car? We can talk about all of this on the way."

They got to the commissary about five that afternoon. Asa Jr. and John were there along with Aunt Maggie, John's wife, who was getting

ADJUSTING | 67

a few groceries. They were all glad to see Asa Sr., and Maggie said, "You just come on over to the house, your room is ready. We'll be glad to have you with us for a while. You need to be out here instead of in town."

John said "Yes, would make it easier on me so we can take care of business."

Asa didn't respond to this, but instead remarked to Asa Jr., "I believe ya grown six inches while I was away. Responsibility must be agreeing with ya."

"Shore did, Pa. I would rather take care of things here than go to school any day."

"Well, go up to the house now and ask your ma if Mr. Lester Moore and I can come up and talk to her. She and I have some business to settle up."

Asa Jr. left immediately and went up to the house. Ma was in the dining room working on a quilt that she had started to help keep her mind occupied. "Ma, Pa is back. He's down at the commissary with a Mr. Lester Moore and wants to know if they can come up to see you on business."

Ma replied, "Well, I guess so; there's things have to be discussed."

Asa Jr. asked, "Ma, what things? Pa is home; ain't that good enough?"

"Asa Jr., you know me and your pa are separated, and now he has got a divorce. There is settling up to do." Ada's voice was strained.

"Ma, you mean Pa ain't never coming home?"

"Not here, he ain't. He may be goin' home to Lillie for all I know."

"Oh, Ma!"

"Oh, Asa Jr., go! Tell them I will see them."

When Asa Jr. left, Ada got up, pulled off her apron and went to her bedroom. She brushed her hair and changed into a navy blue dress, to look her best for what she considered a dreadful occasion. She did, however, hope it would be an amicable meeting. In about ten minutes she heard a knock at the door. Inez ran to the door and immediately started screaming, "Ma, Pa's home!"

Asa gave her a big hug, and said, "I am here to see your ma."

About this time Ada entered the hall and from the doorway. She said in a cool calculated voice, "Come in gentlemen," and ushered them into to the living room on the right. "Please, have a seat." Then she sat down in a chair by the fireplace. Inez had parked herself right next to Asa.

Ada cleared her throat and said, "Inez, go to your room and finish your lessons for school."

Asa reinforced Ada. "Mind your ma. We have things to talk about that children don't need to be here for." After she left the room, Asa got up and closed the door.

Lester Moore said, "Mrs. Stall, we may as well get down to the matter at hand. Asa and I have just come from Upshaw's office, and we are aware of what you want from Asa in order to agree to the Hot Springs divorce."

Ada said, "I see:"

Lester tried to continue, but Asa interrupted and said, "Ada, the long and short of it is I will agree to what ya want, but we have to decide on which farms will satisfy your wishes."

"I see," Ada said again. "Well, I have given this a lot of thought, and there is a little more that I want, which I will tell you after we agree on the property. I want Asa Jr. to have this house with the understanding that I can live here as long as I live. I want Elizabeth to have the Avery Johnson farm, and since it does not have a suitable house on it, I want you to buy the house she is renting in Waycross. I want Inez to have the Arthur Harton farm and house to be hers when she is 21. I want you to pay Jeff Upshaw's fees since you caused all this."

"In addition, I want to be able to get my supplies and groceries from the commissary at no charge and for you to maintain the Delco plant and maintain this house just like it is as long as I live here. You may continue to use the equipment here, the barns and all just as you do now."

"Asa, even though you have done me wrong, I believe you will be honest with these properties and my own farms from my pa, to run them for me and turn over the profits to me."

Asa looked a little stunned. He had no idea this woman to whom he had once been married could come up with all of this. He looked at Lester Moore and said, "It's a deal. Draw up the papers and get with Upshaw so this divorce mess will be over and I can get back to business."

Then Ada said, "There is one more thing. When you come here to see the children you are never to bring Lillie to this house again!"

Asa replied, "No problem. I ain't even seen Lillie in over 2 months no how."

As Asa Sr. and Lester got up to leave, Ada said, "Let me know when the papers are ready. I'll go to Upshaw's and sign them. I wish you the best of luck, Asa."

After they left, Ada collapsed into a chair in the living room. *Well that is that. Thank God, I made it through that without breaking down.* Then she began to cry.

After a few minutes Inez and Asa Jr. came in, and she did her best to explain everything to them before she went to fix supper for the household. There were the three of them and Ivan, Uncle John's boy, this evening. He was Asa Jr.'s age and had been staying with them since Asa went to Little Rock. They also had a boarder at the time, Mrs. Patterson, the schoolteacher.

After about two weeks passed, John came to the house and said he had a letter for Ada from Jeff Upshaw. She opened it. It instructed her to come down on Monday and said the deeds and other papers from Asa were ready.

As usual Ada had Asa Jr. drive her to Upshaw's office. Asa had already signed the papers. With Ada's signature the divorce and settlement were finalized, but it still had to be approved by the judge. There was one possible problem that could come in the future. Ada had never officially filed for a divorce with the court.

FIFTEEN

New Beginnings

Asa Sr. went back to work in earnest to make up for the time he had lost during the separation and divorce. The crops were good, and the turpentine prices were good, so he was pleased with business. He did not see Lillie during this time for several reasons, but mainly because George Harton's lawsuit against him was not settled.

Lillie did write to him about how sorry she was he had so many problems because of her. She always told him that she wished she could be near to comfort him. It seemed that she had no intention of letting him forget about her. She had an objective; she would be his wife as soon as she could.

In November the trial for alienation of affection finally came to court. It lasted two days. George Harton and his attorney, Jim Landers, called several witnesses who all told about Asa's car being seen at George and Lillie's house when George wasn't home. Lottie testified about seeing Lillie in Asa's arms by the icehouse at Elizabeth's wedding.

When Asa was called to testify, he said nothing had happened. He admitted enjoying Lillie's company, but said it was never suggested by either of them that they get together. Then Lillie was called. She stated that she left George because he was mean and abusive to her and the children, that her decision had nothing to do with Asa.

The upside of the whole matter was that George Harton lost the case and wound up looking mighty foolish. Still most folks suspected that there was really more to the story than what came to light in the trial. It was like John had said in the beginning. When there is that much smoke there is bound to be a fire.

Folks didn't have to wait long to find out that was true. A year later Asa Sr. and Lillie were married. The marriage brought another lawsuit by George Harton. He and his lawyer tried to make a case that this marriage was new evidence that Asa had broken up his marriage. He lost again.

Lillie was a very attractive woman. She was well mannered and versed in the ways of the world. She knew how to cook, decorate, and entertain. Asa Sr. had succumbed to all of her charms, and he also knew that her talent and charm would be helpful as he forged ahead with his business pursuits. Indeed, Asa Sr. survived two lawsuits and a divorce and continued to build a very successful business life.

When they first married, Asa Sr. and Lillie lived in a tenant house on the farm. Within six months Asa had built them a new house about a mile from where he had constructed the original house, commissary and turpentine still. Lillie went to great lengths to finish the house in what was a grand manner for the time. All of her furniture came from Savannah, Jacksonville, and Waycross. She bought nothing locally because what she wanted was not available there.

The parlor had a three piece set with a pierced, carved mahogany frame and a mahogany drop front skirting. She completed these pieces with a piano. The latest framed paintings were hung along with gilt framed mirrors. All the furniture was new and was the finest quality one could purchase.

For the dining room, Lillie again chose mahogany for the table, eight chairs, a buffet, and a large break front china cabinet. She also acquired a set of china, crystal, and sterling silver flatware. In one of the bedrooms she had a canopy bed with dresser, chest and nightstand. To her credit she did use her talent to make the window coverings and draperies herself. Needless to say, all of this extravagance was highly criticized by the rest of the Stall family. When Ada heard about all this, she, and the children, too, had plenty of unkind comments about the no good woman who had robbed them of their pa and husband.

Two years after the marriage Lillie was pregnant. She and Asa Sr. had a boy whom they named Joseph. Lillie felt more secure with the marriage after this and hoped the child would make the bond between the two of them even stronger.

By then most of the members of Asa's family had come around to accept Lillie as the new Mrs. Stall since it looked like it was going to be a permanent thing. Lillie was actually a very likeable person and did plenty of nice things for people, so it was difficult to be unfriendly or unkind to her. She even made an attempt at conversation with Asa's three older children when she saw them at the commissary. However, she made little progress with them. They only spoke when spoken to. Ada and her family referred to Joseph as the bastard child, and they referred to him as such when talking to Inez, Asa Jr., and Elizabeth so that they called him the little bastard brother.

All of this bothered Lillie and Asa Sr., but otherwise, life was good. Asa made more and more money and acquired more and more land. Lillie entertained with lunch or dinner for his business associates from Savannah and Jacksonville. All the men found her most pleasant as a hostess.

When Asa Sr. went to Jacksonville or Savannah on business, Lillie often went along. It was on these trips that she would visit the fine stores and make sketches of their dresses. Then she would buy fabric and make them for herself. Lillie was not one to wear long sleeves, go without makeup, and not style her hair. Asa Sr. liked the way she was stylish, and in spite of all the criticism, he was quite pleased with his new wife and family.

However, he never forgot his first wife and family and diligently looked after their needs. When a new car was needed, he bought it for them. When the house Ada and Asa Jr. lived in needed a repair or painting, he saw to it that was done. He was equally responsible with his daughters, an attentive and loving pa. Asa's reality was that he had two families to worry about and take care of, and while he felt it was a lot, he seemed to relish handling it and thrived in so doing.

SIXTEEN
Growing Pains

Asa Jr. decided to quit school after ninth grade and go to work full time for Asa Sr. Even though he owned his own farm now under the terms of the divorce settlement between his parents, working for his pa left him time to chauffer his ma and baby sister, Inez, wherever they wanted to go, as well time for himself.

One of Asa Jr.'s jobs was to go with the truck that was sent to move in new turpentine hands or tenant farmers. He would jokingly tell his ma that he was going to spread chinches today. Chinches were bed bugs or mites that people had in their beds and covers, and were not uncommonly found among the poor such as the turpentine hands and tenant farmers. These workers didn't have much – maybe a bed, a chest, a table, some straight chairs, a wood cook stove and a few pots, pans, and dishes that were usually glazed tin ware. Drinking glasses were fruit jars. However, while there was not a lot of money, if hands worked for Asa Sr., they did not go hungry, and they did make a little extra money when the crops were sold if the harvest was good.

Being fifteen and already owning a car as well as being the son of Asa, Sr., one of the wealthiest men in the county, made Asa Jr. very popular among the young girls of the community. Filling his personal time was not hard. Although this was during the Depression, the commissary had a gas pump, and Asa Sr. allowed his son all the gas he wanted, so getting fuel was easy. Since part of Asa Jr.'s job was running errands for his pa, this gas was just justified as part of the farm and store business expenses.

The gas advantage meant that many Saturday afternoons and Sundays Asa Jr. and one of his male cousins spent their time picking up the girls and going riding. Sometimes there would be a holiday such as Fourth of July when they would plan a picnic. For instance, the O'Quinn girls would make up a picnic basket, and all of them would drive to the rocks at Braxton, Georgia, to the springs for an afternoon of fun.

Many social activities revolved around church. On Sunday mornings Asa Jr. drove Ma and Inez to church, and there some nice young lady would invite him home with her for Sunday dinner. No doubt she expected that this would mean a ride in his car that afternoon. Of course many mothers thought this young man would make a good catch for a son-in-law. Asa, Sr. always cautioned his son to be careful and not get the girls in a family way, "cause if you do you're gonna marry her whether you want to or not!"

While Asa Jr. was busy courting, Asa, Sr. continued acquiring land, eventually owing more than 9,000 acres. During the Depression many small farms sold out, some of the owners going to work for Asa. He had the capital available to provide seed and fertilizer and the commissary for food, and he never turned people away when they came for food. The amounts were charged by the bookkeeper on the ledger and they worked against what they owed. However, many of the accounts were never paid because some people just gave up moved away. So the early 1930s moved on into the mid-1930s, and both of Asa Sr.'s families continued to do fine.

SEVENTEEN

New Girl

Out of school, working full time, and socializing with all the girls, led Asa Jr. to start thinking about marriage and a family, but although he knew a number of fine girls, one had not yet caught his fancy. Then one spring Sunday morning when he took Ma and Inez to church, it happened. Just as they arrived, Bud Gardner's surrey was pulling up to the hitching post, carrying two of his daughters and someone else, someone Asa Jr. didn't know. Who was she?

After church Asa Jr. asked the Myers brothers who the unknown girl with Bud Gardner was. They told him that she was Velma Tyler, Bud's granddaughter.

Cecil Myers asked him, "Do ya wanna meet her?"

Asa Jr. was excited. "Well, shore I do! She's right purty."

Cecil said, "Take your ma home and come back over after lunch. We can go over for a visit to Mr. Gardner's with our sister, Myra. I think Velma's visitin' over there for a week or two."

Asa Jr. took Ma home and ate lunch with her. After lunch he told her he was going for a ride but didn't say where he was going. Asa Jr. arrived at the Myers place a little after two in the afternoon. Cecil and Myra got in his the car, and they all rode over to the Gardner homestead.

When they arrived everybody was sitting on the porch rocking. The three of them piled out of the car and started up to the gate. Mr. Gardner called out, "Howdy. Ya'll come on up a set a spell."

They shuffled up onto the porch, and Cecil said, "Y'all know Asa Stall, Jr. from church."

Mr. Gardner said, "Yep. He is Asa Stall, Sr. and Addie Horton's son from up near Satilla."

They passed a few pleasantries with Bud Gardner and his daughters until finally Mr. Gardner asked, "Have y'all met my granddaughter, Velma Tyler?"

Asa Jr. replied "Sir, I have not, but Cecil and Myra speak mighty highly of her."

Mr. Gardner explained to Asa Jr. that Velma was the daughter of his deceased daughter, Maude. "Her daddy is Saul Tyler, and they live about ten miles down toward Baxley. She comes to see us as often as we can get her here."

Asa Jr. asked, "Well, could Velma go for a ride with us? We'll be careful and won't be late."

"Okay, but you better be careful; you know we don't own one of them things yet." Mr. Gardner gestured toward the Model T. "We still depend on our horse and surrey."

Asa Jr. reassured him that they would be extra careful. The boys rode in the front and the girls in the back.

Cecil said, "Let's drive down to the creek near the wash hole." That was an area of the creek where everybody liked to swim.

All agreed that sounded like a good idea, and so they headed for the creek where they parked under a tree and got out of the car. They stayed in the shade just talking and passing the afternoon for a little while until suddenly Cecil announced, "I've got to go home, got chores to do. Gotta feed the hogs, and Myra's gotta tend to the chickens."

Asa Jr. looked at Velma. "Is it okay if we take 'em home before I take ya back?"

"Well, I guess so."

Asa and Velma dropped off the Myers and started toward the Gardner place. Asa Jr. asked Velma how old she was, and she told him that she was fifteen, but would be turning sixteen in June. Then she asked Asa Jr. if he was still in school.

"No; I quit in ninth grade and went to work for Pa. His farm's 'bout ten miles down the road in Appling County."

"Oh," Velma said. Then she went on. "I come to Grandpa and Grandma's as often as I can. My aunts are real good to me, getting me cloths and shoes. You know my mama died when I was just four years old; my little sister died when she was three, and my brother died when he was ten."

"That's real sad; ya must be all alone with your pa."

"Well no cause he got married again, and has got five more children by this wife, my stepmother. I don't like her very much, and there's so many of us there ain't hardly enough to go 'round. I think that's why my real mama's sisters do so much for me." Then she looked at Asa and asked, "Asa where do you live?"

"I live with my ma and baby sister. Ma and Pa divorced, and so I live with Ma, but the house and farm are mine from Pa when they got divorced."

They were almost to the Gardner Place, so Asa Jr. said, "I'd shore like to see ya again. Will ya be at church next Sunday?"

"Don't know if my daddy will let me come back then or not. He says Grandpa and his people spoil me and put big ideas in my head."

Asa Jr. thought for a minute and then said, "Well could I come down to see ya at your place on Saturday afternoon about three, and we could go to the picture show?"

"You don't know where I live."

"You can tell me. Are ya going home today?"

"I think I have to 'cause my Aunt Martha has a car, and mostly she takes me home on her way back to Alma."

"When we get back, I'll ask if I can take ya home so I'll know where you stay, and then I can come calling." Asa Jr. was pleased with his idea.

"Well, you'll have to ask my aunt. If she says it's okay, then you can, and I can introduce you to my daddy and ask about the picture show."

By the time they were coming up to the gate of the Gardner place, Mr. Gardner was back on the porch in his rocker. Asa Jr. noticed that it was getting to be dusk, but no lights were on in his house, and so he realized they didn't have electricity.

Mr. Gardner said, "Did ya have a nice ride?" Then looking beyond them he asked, "Where're the Myers?"

Asa Jr. answered. "They needed to get home and finish some chores, so we dropped 'em off on our way back here."

"Well, Velma, your Aunt Martha's about ready to leave, so ya best get your things together," was Mr. Gardner's response.

Asa Jr. spoke up quickly. " Do ya think I could take Velma home so I can see where she lives? I'd like to take her to the picture show on Saturday."

Mr. Gardner thought on that a bit and finally said, "I guess that'd be okay, ya taking her home. As far as ya calling on Velma to take her to the picture show, that'll be up to her daddy."

Velma went to gather her things, and she and Asa Jr. left.

EIGHTEEN
Smitten

While they were driving, Asa Jr. asked, "What is it ya like 'bout staying at your Grandpa's?"

"It's just so much better than at Daddy's. I wish I could stay there all the time, but my Grandma, who you didn't meet, is sick. She takes to bed a lot. Grandpa is very religious, and every night when he comes in off the porch, he lights the kerosene lamp and reads aloud from the Bible and has prayer before we go to bed."

Velma continued, "It's not as much fun during the week, but some of my aunts come on the weekend. They cook and clean. I collect the eggs in the morning and draw that cold water from the well to the kitchen and back porch. The kitchen's 'cross the back porch from the house in the log room. Sometimes they let me help cook. That's fun. And sometimes Grandma gets up for a short spell, but then she has to go lie back down again."

"What's wrong with her?"

"I believe they say she's got Dropsy (congestive heart failure). She's got swollen eyes and ankles and hands. She don't have much breath neither. Aunt Polly and Aunt Martha said Dr. Sharpe said there wasn't much can be done for her condition."

"Where do ya go to school?"

"I went to Deal School out near my house. I finished eighth grade, but there wasn't no money for books to go no further and besides, there's all the little ones at home to be cared for, so I have to help with them."

Asa Jr. realized that Velma and her family didn't have much at all, not even as much as Granddaddy Gardner, but he didn't care because she was such a pretty little thing, not more than five feet tall with dark curly hair and tiny feet. Yes, Asa Jr. was smitten.

Velma directed him to turn up this narrow lane, and in less then a minute they pulled up in front of her home. It was an unpainted clapboard house, with a dog trot in the middle. A dog trot was a wide open area with a porch at the end of it, rooms on either side of the open space, and a kitchen and eating area on the other side opposite the porch.

It was nearly dark, and Mr. Tyler was on the porch. Asa Jr. could see kerosene lamps lit inside. Mr. Tyler said, "Who's this bringing ya home, Velma? I was expecting your Aunt Martha to drop you off." He sounded a little gruff.

"Daddy," Velma replied, "this here is Asa Stall, Jr. from the Satilla Community up near Zora. He was at church this morning and came over to Grandpa's with the Myers this afternoon. He offered to bring me on home."

"Um," grunted Mr. Tyler. "I know of that family, turpentine folks with lots of timber."

Asa Jr. responded, "Well I guess that's one way to think of us." When Mr. Tyler didn't say anymore, Asa Jr. said, "Well I reckon I best be gettin' home before Ma thinks I'm lost. Nice to meet ya, Mr. Tyler. Uh, and I wanted to ask, Sir, would it be okay if I called on Velma next Saturday after dinner around 3 o'clock and took her to the picture show?"

Mr. Tyler scratched his head and looked at Velma, "Do ya wanna to go?"

"Oh yes, Daddy! I've only ever been to one picture with Aunt Polly and Uncle Jonah down in Baxley."

"Well I'll let ya go then. Rich folks with cars can do them kinda things. Takes all day to get over to Baxley and back with the horse and buggy."

"Well, Velma, I reckon I better go; I'll see ya Saturday. Thank you, Mr. Tyler, for lettin' me come calling."

NINETEEN
First Date

Asa Jr. went to work on Monday taking care of the list of chores his pa had for him. He hauled corn from one of the tenant farm corn cribs to the mule barn corn crib; then he put some corn in the cow barn to be used to feed the milk cows. Then there were the two cows, the Guernsey and the Holstein, to milk. His ma still mixed the milk.

All week while Asa Jr. was keeping up with all the chores to be done, he kept thinking about his date coming up on Saturday. The week seemed to drag by, but Saturday morning finally came. Asa Jr. finished his chores, but then Ma wanted to go to town to get a few things. He was feeling a little impatient then, but he said, "Okay, but I have a date with Velma Tyler this afternoon to go the picture show in Baxley."

"Oh, who's she?" inquired his ma.

"She's Mr. Bud Gardner's granddaughter. I saw her at church last Sunday. The Myers introduced me to her after church, and that afternoon after we all went ridin', and I took her home and asked her pa if I could come calling." Asa Jr. was nearly breathless from saying all that so fast.

His ma just looked at him. "Have you told your pa about this girl?"

"No, I didn't think I needed to mention it 'cause I am off on this Saturday anyway."

Nothing more was said about his date as they went into town. Ada did her shopping, picking out a new dress from Mrs. Hirsh at Hirsh Clothing Store, and they returned home around one o'clock.

Ma pulled out some leftovers, and as they ate lunch, she said, "Don't reckon you'll be home for supper."

"Don't spect so."

"Well I gotta cook anyway; your sister Elizabeth'll be here in a while with her family."

Asa Jr. got dressed and excitedly set out for his first date with Velma Tyler. He figured it would take about half an hour to get to her place, and he made good time, arriving at straight up three o'clock.

Mr. Tyler was walking up from the field in his work clothes.

"How are ya, Sir?" Asa inquired.

"Fair to middling I reckon, hot from plowing, needed to get some cold water from the well. Ya want a drink?"

"No thanks; I just finished a quart of iced tea before I left to come here."

"Oh, I see y'all have ice, too."

It seemed to Asa Jr. that the Tylers were little better off than his and his pa's tenant farmers, even though they did own their small farm. *Oh well; they seemed nice, and Velma was so pretty.*

As Asa Jr. was looking around the place, Velma came out on the porch dressed in a poke-a-dot voile dress. *Wow! She looks wonderful* was all he could think, but he didn't compliment her.

Velma smiled shyly and said, "I'm ready."

She waited for Asa Jr. to help her into the car, and then they headed off to the picture show. At first there wasn't much conversation as if they didn't know what to say to each other, but finally Asa Jr. managed to say, "You sure do look pretty in that dress today."

"Why, thank you. Aunt Polly made it for me. 'Member, I told you my aunts make most of my clothes. But Daddy says it makes me think I'm better then the rest of 'em."

Velma hit a talking streak then. "I don't like my step ma. I wish Daddy hadn't married her and kept me at home. Aunt Martha doesn't have children; she wanted me to come live with her when my mama died, but Daddy wouldn't let me. He said I had to stay with him and help. We ain't got enough for so many. Sometimes I think about runnin' away, but I don't know where I'd go, and if I had to come back to Daddy's then it would be even worse after me runnin' away."

Asa Jr. wasn't sure how to respond, so he just said, "It don't sound like ya got the best situation in the world, but we'll just have some fun today - take your mind off them conditions."

They reached the theater in Baxley. A Lone Ranger picture was the movie for the day, and it had a showing at four o'clock. Asa Jr. purchased the tickets, and they went on inside and got popcorn and fresh lemonade.

Velma told Asa Jr. that she needed to sit pretty close to the front because she couldn't see well from the back. "I probably need glasses, but ain't no money for that."

They sat down just as the movie started, and enjoyed their snacks during the first few minutes. Then about half way through the movie Asa Jr. reached out for Velma's hand. When she responded with a squeeze of his hand, he felt sparks.

When the movie was over about six o'clock, Velma reminded Asa Jr. that she could not stay out past nine. If she did her daddy would be mad and not let her go again.

"That's okay," Asa Jr. responded. "I have to get home so I can get up early and take Ma and Inez to church in the morning. Will ya be at church tomorrow?"

"No." We'll go to the Methodist church tomorrow 'cause all the Tylers are Methodist." Then she added, "I'd rather be Baptist cause Grandpa and Grandma says them Methodists ain't been baptized, that they just had a little water sprinkled on their head and that ain't good enough."

Asa Jr. chuckled slightly at this. "So ya'd rather be Baptist ya think?"

"Oh yes, and I've been baptized in the Baptist church down at Zora Creek. I spent revival week with Grandpa two years ago, and I got saved and baptized. My Daddy wasn't too happy, but it was done."

Asa Jr. decided to change the subject. "Well, did ya like the picture?"

"Oh yes. I wish I could get to go to the picture show more, but I read as much as I can. Aunt Martha brings me books. Do you read Asa?"

"Naw, not much, never really interested me."

They were back at the Tyler place; Asa Jr. opened the door and let Velma out. They said good night, but then Asa asked about the next weekend. "Saturday could I pick ya up about ten? Then we could pick up my cousin and his girlfriend and go to Braxton to the rocks for a picnic. I'm pretty sure I could get Ma and Pearl to fix us a basket.

Velma smiled, not so shyly this time. "I am sure it'll be okay, but if it ain't, I'll pitch a hissy fit, and then I'll get to go."

TWENTY

Big Development

This time the week went fast for Asa Jr. as he looked forward to Saturday with Velma. He asked his cousin, Alvin, if he and Irene Palmer would like to go for a picnic on Saturday to the rocks. Alvin was all for it and he was pretty sure Irene could go. Asa Jr. asked his pa if he could have off on Saturday to go on a picnic with Alvin and Irene.

Asa Sr. said, "Yes if you got all your work done by then," and, remembering when he was his son's age, he added, "Who ya takin'?"

"Velma Tyler; she's Mr. Bud Gardner's granddaughter, the Gardners from over at Zora."

"How long ya been seeing her?"

"Not long, but she shore is purty."

"Pretty on the outside don't always mean pretty on the inside. Let me tell ya something, Son; them folks ain't like us. They're more like our tenant farmers, kinda hand to mouth livin'. I know of the Tylers, however, and havin' money don't make you a better person. From what I know, I think they are some good people."

Asa Jr. said, "'Specially the Gardners. They're real good to Velma."

"But now, Son, you be careful; you'd be a mighty good catch for them, if you understand me."

"Pa I ain't gonna git caught. I'm just going for a ride and a picnic."

"I know, but 'member what I've told ya," replied his pa.

When Saturday morning came, ma fixed up a picnic basket with fried chicken, biscuits, deviled eggs, potato salad, chocolate cake and some sweet iced tea. Asa Jr. got ice out of the ice house and loaded up the trunk. He and Alvin picked up Irene and then went on to Velma's. They got there a few minutes after ten.

Velma was already waiting on the porch wearing a yellow sun dress and a straw hat. Asa Jr. said, "Ya shore do look mighty fixed up in the straw hat."

Velma flashed him a big smile. "Aunt Polly got it for me; she says a girl ought never to get sun on her face or arms. That's why I brought my voile jacket, wouldn't want to get all freckled now." She smiled again.

The pair really made a sight. Asa Jr. was big and awkward, and Velma was just a tiny little thing. Asa Jr. introduced her to Alvin and Irene, and they headed for Braxton, again the girls in the back, the boys in the front, as was customary.

It took about an hour and a half to get to the rocks. When they tumbled out of the car, Alvin said, "Let's got for a walk." He and Irene headed off for the spring.

Asa Jr. and Velma climbed up to the top of the rocks and looked down. Asa Jr. was holding Velma's hand when she stumbled on a rock. He caught her, and before she knew what had happened, he had smacked a big kiss on her.

Velma said, "Well, lordy didn't you take my breath away!"

"Shore was nice," was all Asa Jr. said.

Velma was flushed. It was hard to know if it was a little embarrassment or a little excitement, but on the way back down Asa Jr. held her hand tightly.

When they all meet back at the car around noon, Asa Jr. said, "I'm starved let's eat!"

They spread out a blanket under a tree and opened up the box of food. Asa Jr. got out the ice and the cooler. Pretty soon the food and the noon warmth, made them a little sleepy.

Alvin said, "Time for a nap", and he proceeded to lay his head in Irene's lap. She leaned back against the tree, and they both closed their eyes.

Asa Jr. followed Alvin's moves and laid his head in Velma's lap. She leaned back against the cooler. Suddenly she started running her fingers through his curly brown hair. That surprised him, and he said, "Don't stop; that feels real good, like I could get used to it."

Velma said, "Bet you could, but I wouldn't want anybody else to do it."

Asa Jr. was puzzled. "Well why not?"

"Well 'cause you're special to me."

"And yore special to me, too." Asa Jr. piped up. "Heck, I'd like to see more of ya- like every day."

Velma giggled. "Well, I don't think that's possible."

That's when Asa Jr. blurted out his first thought. "It would be if we got hitched."

"Oh my! Asa Stall Jr., are you asking me to marry you?"

"Well, yup I guess I am."

"I think I would like that."

Asa Jr. jumped up and pulled her into his arms for one long embrace and kiss. "I will ask your pa soon as we get back."

"No you will not! I will tell Daddy myself what I am doing."

"Oh." Asa Jr. was stunned by her reply. This should have been a warning to him about what the future with a strong willed woman might look like, but in his youthful exuberance, he gave it no more thought.

Velma asked, "Where would we live?"

"With Ma. The house belongs to me; 'member, I told ya 'bout gettin' it in the divorce settlement."

BIG DEVELOPMENT | 91

"In that case, I guess I had better meet you ma sometime soon."

All the animated voices caught Alvin and Irene's attention. "What's all the excitement about?" Alvin wanted to know.

Asa Jr. exclaimed, "Velma's agreed to marry me!"

After a moment of stunned silence, Alvin said "When?"

"Sometime in June."

"Ooo, we wanna be there," Irene said.

Velma said, "Well of course y'all have to be there; 'specially since y'all are the first to know."

Asa Jr. admonished everybody. "Don't say nothin' about this to nobody. I gotta talk to Pa."

Alvin laughed. "Yea, ya better 'cause ya work for him and he's got the money."

Velma frowned. "You don't have to ask your pa's permission!"

"Uh, well no, but I want him to approve."

"Well, I don't care if my daddy approves or not! He didn't ask me if he could marry again, and I will just tell him what I intend to do."

Irene was startled. "Well I sure wouldn't try that with my pa!"

They took Velma home about six o'clock. Asa Jr. said, "When can I see ya again?"

"Wednesday you can pick me up and we will go for a ride – if you like."

On the way home after dropping Velma off, Alvin commented, "Velma is awfully strong willed."

"Oh, she'll be okay once we get married and are settled down," was Asa Jr.'s assured response.

Alvin couldn't help but say, "I ain't so sure about that."

TWENTY ONE

Getting Crowded

The weeks flew by for Asa Jr. and Velma. Both were very excited about the prospect of their new life together. They decided to wait to make the big announcement until after Velma could meet Asa Jr.'s family, and he could meet her aunts, Polly and Martha. As soon as this was done, Asa Jr. told his pa he wanted to get married to Velma.

Pa replied, "You're 3 x 7 now, Son, so you're a grown man, but I hope ya know what you're doin'."

"Pa she's real nice – and so pretty too."

"Yup, she's pretty, but she's young and ya don't know her very well, and ya know less of her family. You're not well matched as far as family backgrounds, but ya can make your own decisions, and if this is what you're determined to do, then I wish ya the best. For a weddin' present, I'll give ya $500.00."

"Thanks, Pa; that's real generous."

"When is this hitchin' to be?"

"Sometime in June."

Velma also informed her family of the pending marriage. All Grandpa Gardner wanted to know was, "Well, is he a church goer?"

"Oh yes," Velma assured him. "He's at Zora all the time."

Aunt Polly and Aunt Martha gave their blessings and supported

Velma's decision by getting some clothes together for her. They wanted be sure she had a few nice clothes to carry with her when she got married, and they knew her daddy wouldn't able to do anything for her. They decided on six dresses as well as what she would wear for the wedding. For that Aunt Martha got her a cream dress and matching hat and white shoes with a bow.

Asa Jr. and Velma settled on June 20th, a Saturday, for the wedding date. They didn't tell anybody else except Alvin and Irene who would go with them, and one other person. Asa Jr. shared the details with his pa, and he asked him if he could be off on the following Monday, Tuesday, and Wednesday for a little wedding trip.

"Well, okay," Pa said, "but ya ought to be working now that you're gonna have a wife!"

On June 20th, Asa Jr. Stall and Velma Tyler, accompanied by Alvin and Irene, headed over to Denton. There the Justice of the Peace married them. After that they took Alvin and Irene back home and left for a trip to Silver Springs, Florida. On the way out of town, they stopped by Asa Jr.'s house and informed his ma that they had just gotten married.

Ma said, "Ain't surprised since you brought her to dinner three times from church. You never did that with Pearl Horton." She turned to Velma and just said, "Welcome to the family. Y'all can have the front room so you'll have some privacy."

Asa Jr. said, "Thanks, but we're goin' on a little trip right now. We'll be back on Wednesday."

Ma asked with some surprise, "Where ya goin' and does your pa approve?"

"He said I could be off on Monday, Tuesday and Wednesday. We're goin' down to Silver Springs, Florida."

"I've heard it's real pretty down there. Y'all be careful. I'll see ya when you get back."

Asa Jr. and Velma set out on their new life together. They stopped in Folkston, Georgia, at a small motel for their first night of married life. Asa Jr. discovered Velma was not experienced and was scared, a virgin he guessed, and he liked that idea. He calmed her down, took things slowly and the beginning of a long, if not always easy, marriage was consummated.

Sunday morning the newlyweds got up and continued the drive to Silver Springs. They had not been on the road long before Velma demanded, "What's this about you and Pearl Horton? Were you gonna marry her? I know her. Y'all are the same age. I've seen her at Zora. Did she run her fingers through your hair, too?"

Asa Jr. said, "No, and I married you. I did see her some, but didn't mean nothin', so now don't ya go gettin' all jealous over it. I married you, and I don't have eyes for nobody else."

They stopped in Callahan, Florida, for breakfast and then drove the last miles to Silver Springs. There they rented a cabin and shared some intimate time before going out to see the sights. When it was supper time, they ate at the park restaurant.

Monday morning they enjoyed the unique view from the glass bottom boats. After that they went to Ocala to the amusement park where they rode the Ferris wheel and other rides and played some of the midway games. some of the midway games. Asa Jr. really wanted to win his new bride a prize. His desire was met with success when he won a Shirley Temple doll for knocking over milk bottles with a ball. The school girl in Velma was thrilled to get the doll and was very proud of her new husband's success.

Despite how much fun they were having, and how attentive to her Asa Jr. was being, Velma just could not help saying, "I'm glad I got this pretty doll instead of Pearl Horton … and I got you too!"

"There ya go again. Forget about Pearl Horton. I don't wanna here no more about her." Asa Jr. was annoyed. He found himself hoping that she wasn't going to be jealous and possessive their whole married life, and he recalled Alvin's comment from the day of the picnic.

Tuesday morning they got up early and started back home. They decided to drive straight through on the return trip, and so it was about dark when they arrived Tuesday night.

"Are you hungry?" Ma asked.

Asa Jr. said, "Yes. Been drivin' all day with barely a stop for a bite."

"Well I have some leftovers on the pie shelf. I'll fix you a plate."

"I'll help you," offered Velma.

"I can manage on my own thank you."

Inez came in off the back porch. "Did y'all have a good time? What all did ya see?"

Velma replied, "Oh we had a wonderful time," but before she could add any details Inez chimed in with her news.

"I'm going away to college in August. Pa's sending me to the Georgia's Women's College in Milledgeville."

Ma had returned to the room. "Yes, he thinks it's a good idea. Your sister has been seeing George Gosley, and her pa hopes she can do better than that."

Inez wailed. "Oh, Ma, he's so handsome and really polite, a gentleman!"

"Well maybe so, but his family's bootleggers."

Inez pouted. "Ma, now ya don't know that for sure."

"It's common knowledge, Inez!"

Inez changed the subject. "I've got more news for ya, Asa and Velma. I talked Pa into installing us an inside bathroom and to put runnin' water in the house, too. And did ya know that woman he married is expecting a baby!"

Inez would talk awful about her pa and his second family and use very unlady-like words, such as bastard, to describe his child, and then she would go down to the commissary and sit on his lap, wrap him around her little finger and get whatever she wanted.

"Pa just gave me a thousand dollars to go shopping before I go away to college," she bragged.

Asa Jr. laughed. "Well that's small change to get ya out a here, where things will be more peaceful with ya gone 'cause you're always stirring stuff up."

Ma said sharply, "Asa, be nice to your sister!"

Then Ma continued. "I told Cousin Alvin you were gonna get married, and he'd need to find someplace else to live cause we're running out of room. Inez and me will be sharing a room now that you and Velma got the front room. And I have to have a room for Elizabeth when she and my granddaughter come every week-end from Waycross, and she's letting Sally stay the summer with me after next weekend."

Now, as the family member recalling this story, I just have to take a minute before I go on and make an observation here. We had quite a group that was going to be living under one roof, three strong minded women and one man each woman had some claim to in the middle of them. It's often said there is no house big enough for three grown women. In this case it was even truer since Velma was an outsider and taking up all of Asa Jr.'s time. The other women did not particularly like her, and so the situation was going to get very tense.

TWENTY TWO
Medical Emergency

In the weeks following the wedding, Asa Jr. went to work every day, leaving Inez, Ada, and Velma at home together. Household chores now had three women to get them done. The garden vegetables were coming in, and Ma said, "Girls we had better go pick and get some canning done for winter."

"I can't pick vegetables; they make me itch," Inez whined.

Velma volunteered. "I'll pick the vegetables and bring them in."

She donned a long sleeve shirt and a big straw hat. The first day she picked butter beans, and the three of them sat on the porch shelling. The next day she brought in the peas and squash.

Ma supervised the canning. Glass Mason jars were put into a large cooker filled with hot water, just less than boiling, to heat for an hour. After that towels were used to remove them while they were still hot. Jars were then filled with prepared vegetables, leaving just the right amount of headspace for each item being canned, and lids were securely tightened on each one. Next, the jars went back into the hot water which was brought to a rolling boil and covered with a lid. After the required amount of boiling time, the pot was removed from the heat and jars allowed to remain in it for five minutes before being removed and set out to cool. During this time they would form a tight seal which kept the vegetables form spoiling. It was a long, hot process, and with the wood stove fired up, the kitchen got mighty hot, but Velma paid careful attention and learned the process.

Canning went on all summer until the vegetables ran out. After the vegetables were canned, it was time to can fruit. There were peaches from the orchards as well as the fall pears. Additionally, when the blackberries were ripe, the women picked them from the fence rows and made blackberry jelly and jam. All of these canned goods were food staples during the winter months. Between all of the work during the week and church on Sunday, the weeks went by quickly.

Asa Jr., in addition to his usual work, was still driving his ma and Inez when they needed to go somewhere. Velma would go along for the ride. In mid-August they made a trip to Waycross to buy the clothes for Inez to take to college when she left in a few weeks. This was a long day trip, but was necessary to keep Inez happy because Hirsh's Clothing Store in Hazlehurst did not have clothes fine enough to suit her.

Asa Jr. had noticed that, as Velma told him when they first met, she did not see very well, so while they were in Waycross, he took her to see Dr. Wheeler, the best eye doctor in town. Upon examination it was determined that indeed she did need glasses. The doctor told the couple the glasses would be ready in two weeks.

Two weeks later Asa Jr. and Velma went back to Waycross to pick up her glasses. Velma was pleasantly surprised by how differently things looked with them on. Now she could read the signs on the road way, and she thought Asa Jr. looked even more handsome.

Inez, always one to start trouble, said to Velma when she saw her wearing her glasses, "You look an awful lot like an owl with those things on."

Velma retorted, "Well, you don't look any better with or without them on."

Inez screamed, "You're being ugly to me in my own house."

Velma yelled back, "This is not your house! It is Asa's house!"

Inez sneered, "Well I have my own house over at the Arthur Horton Place."

Ma interrupted. "Girls that's enough! Don't wanna here anymore about this. We all live here together so we need to get along."

"Not for long Ma," Inez replied. "I am gonna to move out, and ya can come with me."

Ma reminded her. "You're going away to college, and you won't be doing any other moving any time soon."

Inez had to have the last word. "Don't count on it."

The next morning Velma got up and went in to help Ada with breakfast.

Ada said, "You don't look well."

"Well I do have a pain in my side, started around four o'clock this morning."

"Maybe it's just an upset stomach from something you ate."

However, by the time breakfast was over, the pain had gotten much worse and Velma was doubled over with it. She went to lie down, but it continued to get worse. When Ma went to check on her, Velma told her it was real bad and that she was sick to her stomach, too.

Ma sent Pearl to go find Asa Jr. and tell him to come to the house. He was fixing to go check on some timber for his pa, but he came back to the house instead. His ma told him that Velma was in real bad pain, so he went to the room to check on her. Velma told him how much she hurt and that she felt sick all over.

Ma said, "It might be her appendix. Ya better go into town and get Doc Martin and his nurse."

Asa Jr. did and returned with the doctor in about an hour. Dr. Martin took one look at Velma and said, "I'm sure she has appendicitis, I must operate immediately! Asa, go get my operating table off the back of the truck. Miss Ada, go boil some water as quick as you can."

Dr. Martin went out to his truck to get his medicine bag and utensil bag. He had Asa Jr. set up the operating table in the parlor in the middle of the room. In addition to the Delco light fixtures, the doctor had them raise the shades to get as much extra light as possible into the room. Ada brought in a kettle of boiling water. Dr. Martin poured it over his operating utensils and wiped them off with a cloth soaked in alcohol.

Velma was brought into the parlor, and the men set her on the operating table. Dr. Martin gave her ether to make her sleep, so she would not feel him cutting into her for the appendix removal. It took over an hour to complete the surgery, and the appendix was on the verge of bursting, which, had that happened, could have been fatal. Dr. Martin then stitched up the incision and said he would wait until she came out of the anesthesia before he left. He also said that he would leave the nurse overnight just in case there was a problem.

"She will be very nauseated when she wakes up so be sure to keep a pail by her bed. She needs to stay in bed for at least a week."

When Velma woke up, the doctor took his leave. Asa Jr. asked if she wanted anything. She immediately said she wanted her Aunt Polly to come help look after her.

Ada said, "That's fine. We could use some extra help."

Asa Jr. went to get Aunt Polly, and the appendix was placed in a medicine bottle containing alcohol. Velma kept it the rest of her life.

Before all the commotion started that morning, Inez had walked over to a cousin's house across the branch. When she got home, she asked what was going on. They told her what had happened to Velma.

"It happened 'cause she was so mean to me yesterday," Inez sneered.

Ma said, "Hush your mouth, it coulda been you sick."

TWENTY THREE
Busy Season

Right after Labor Day Inez packed her trunks, and Asa Jr. drove her to Georgia Woman's College in Milledgeville. They got her settled into the dormitory and registered for classes, and Asa Jr. returned home. In just a few days the family received a letter from her. She wrote that she was having a grand time and that the boys from nearby Georgia Military College were such handsome gentlemen.

"We see them on Saturday and Sunday afternoons and Sunday morning at church. Life is so much more exciting then being on the farm," she wrote.

Inez always put on airs, and at college she was haughtily promoting herself as the daughter of a timber baron to whom she was heiress. She had a fine wardrobe thanks to her pa's spoiling generosity. Asa Sr. had hoped that while Inez was away studying at college, she would meet a suitable husband. However, he had no idea that while she was meeting a lot of eligible boys, she was not paying any serious attention to her education. Her ma, however, was reading between the lines, and she quickly figured out that there was very little studying going on. The truth was that Inez, free from the restraints of farm life and Ma and Pa's rules, was only interested in having a good time.

One of the boys she met was Sam Thompson. He was from Baxley, Georgia. She thought he was the most fun to be with, and she wrote to her pa to tell him that she had met a very nice boy and she would like for Pa to meet him over the Thanksgiving break.

This did not go over well at all. Asa Sr. knew of this boy and his family, and he hit the ceiling. He had his bookkeeper write a letter to Inez, and he signed it. He stated emphatically to Inez that those were not her kind of people. He said that they were moon shiners and that liquor money was what paid for that boy to get into the Georgia Military School, that the family was trying to buy him out of trouble. Asa Sr.'s letter further contended that Sam Thompson had already gotten a girl in the family way, but that his family denied it and sent him off to school.

Inez, being the little vixen that she was, found all these details titillating. They just made the boy even more exciting to her. She continued to see Sam but did not mention him again.

Thanksgiving arrived. She came home as planned, and on Saturday she got one of the O'Quinn girls to pick her up. She told Ma she was going to the movies in Baxley and would spend the night with the O'Quinn's. What she actually did when she got to Baxley was to meet Sam. Then the two of them took off in his car and drove down to Jessup where they got married. When Inez came home on Sunday, she told her ma that she was married.

On Monday she and Sam went down to the commissary and told Asa Sr.

Her pa sighed heavily and shook his head. All he said was, "Baby, ya've made your bed; now you'll have to lie in it." Asa Sr. looked tired and unhappy.

Inez gushed to her pa, "But, Pa, I love him. He makes me sooo happy." Then giving him a sweet little girl smile she added, "Pa, I need a little money so we can go on a little trip. Pleeze."

Never able to say no to his youngest, Asa Sr. turned to his bookkeeper. "Give her $100.00 out of the safe."

Money in hand, Inez and Sam left for Jacksonville to spend a few days. When they came back, Inez announced that she would be moving to her house on the Arthur Harton place and that Sam would be working for his pa. When they moved, Inez wanted, rather expected, her ma to move with her, but Ada wanted to stay where she was with Asa Jr. This did not please Inez because, if her ma wouldn't move in with her, then she would have to do all the cooking and cleaning herself, something she had never planned to do. Not only did she want her ma to come do her work for her, but she also wanted to control the money that her ma's farms generated. She figured she had better come up with a plan to get her way.

It occurred to Inez that if she could get a big row started between Velma and her ma, Ma would move. To that end she lied to her ma saying that she had seen Velma flirting with Bo Thompson at the party the Thompson's held for her and Sam. Ma confronted Velma with this. Like Asa Sr., Ada always favored her youngest over anybody else, and so she always believed what Inez said, even if deep inside she knew better. Velma denied the accusation and told Ada that Inez was lying. Well, that did it.

"Don't ya dare call my daughter a liar!"

Velma flared. "That is exactly what I am calling her, a bald face liar. And if you believe her over me then we can't stay under the same roof."

When Asa Jr. got home and heard about what had happened, he just looked at his ma and said, "It just ain't so, Ma. She never left my side at that party."

At that point Velma said, "Asa, let's just get your pa to let us move into one the tenant houses. I can't stay where I'm not believed."

"No," Ma said. "Asa, this is your house. I'll move in with Inez and Sam."

Inez got her way one more time!

As Ada prepared to move out, farm life remained busy. It was time for two big events, cane grinding and hog killing.

The cane grinder was out behind the boiler shelter. It was a machine with two large threaded cylinders very close together. A long pole ran off the center of the top of the mill. Turning this pole rotated the cylinders to grind the juices out of the cane. The pole was turned by a tethered mule walking around in a circle. Stalks of sugar cane were pushed into the center of the cylinder which forced the juice out of the cane. The juice then ran down a trough into a barrel. It did not take long for the juice barrel to get full. The full barrel was then removed and poured into the boiler until the boiler was about three quarters full. While the boiler full of juices was being cooked into syrup, the grinding process stopped.

As the juices boiled, a skim would rise to the top; this cane skim would be dipped off. The syrup maker watched the cane juices until it cooked down and thickened to just the right consistency to be syrup. If it cooked too long it would become brown sugar crystals. When the syrup was ready, workers would dip it out of the boiler into syrup buckets which were really just tin pails. Farmers and turpentine hands often carried their lunches in syrup buckets.

There were usually one or two people in the neighborhood who were syrup makers. Syrup making was a fun time on the farm with most of the small farms using the boiler at Asa Jr.'s house. His grinder was the one built by his pa, Asa Sr., for his farm. Syrup making time was a social event with folks gathering in the evening, often around a wash tub full of boiling peanuts, while they shared the latest gossip.

The other event that happened at this time of year and was centered in the boiler shelter was hog killing. Hog killing usually took place after the first frost in the fall. The weather needed to be cooler so the bugs and flies were less of a problem. The ritual started early, around 4:00 A.M.

The hogs were kept in a pen across the road from the boiler shelter. They were shot in the head with a rifle and then dragged across the road on a sled pulled by a mule. There the carcasses were tossed in the boiler of hot water. After boiling, they were laid on a table made of 2x8 boards and saw horses. Here the bristles were scrapped away with a wire brush and knife. Next they were taken out back of the shelter and hung up on a pole with a cross bar where they were gutted. The hog guts, known as chitlins, were set aside to be cleaned by the black women from the quarters who were very skilled at this operation. Better and stronger gut sections were kept to use for sausage casings.

After all of this was done, the hogs were carried back to the table under the shelter where they were cut up into quarters. Fat skin was removed, cut into small pieces, and placed back in the boiler where it was cooked into lard. The liquid fat was dipped into ten gallon lard cans and sealed for storage. It was used later for frying, baking and seasoning in vegetables as well as in cakes and breads.

As the fat cooked away, the outside skin would remain. This skin by-product become what was known as cracklins (pork rind).The cracklins left in the boiler were placed into a cracklins squeezer, a round cylinder with a top connected to a large screw. The cylinder had a hand crank which came down on the cracklins and squeezed out the last lard. This left only the pig skins behind.

There was no waste in the hog killing process. All of the hog was used; shoulders, hams and bacon were taken to the smoke house to be cured with salt. Pork chops and ribs were put in the ice house and were eaten first. The cured pork was saved for winter. Any pieces remaining were ground into sausage meat to be stuffed into the hog guts and smoked for use later. The pig feet were boiled; the head meat was removed, seasoned, placed in a flower sack, and hung in the smoke house for all the excess grease to drip out. This process left the meat compact enough to be sliced and eaten. It was called souse meat. The brains from the hog, considered a delicacy, were put in the ice house or ice box and later scrambled with eggs for the morning breakfast.

(Note: After Velma's Aunt Martha died of a brain tumor, Velma no longer allowed pig brains in the house. Nor would she allow fried chitlins.)

TWENTY FOUR
Heir

In tandem with all the on-going fall farm work, Ada got moved in with Inez and Sam. That meant that Asa Jr. and Velma had some furniture shopping to do. They went to Hazlehurst to Jarmon and Hammock Hardware and to Wilson's Hardware and bought two bedroom suites and a bed. In truth, Velma was relieved to finally have some furniture of her own. Ma had left the porch furniture along with the living room set and the dinning room furniture.

By Christmas Velma was pregnant. This caused much excitement in her family, and Asa, Sr. was mighty pleased and hoping for the first male grandchild. The pregnancy went well during the winter and spring. The baby was due in July. Babies were delivered at home assisted by the town doctor or a midwife.

When Velma went into labor, Asa Jr. sent for Dr. Martin. He came out in an hour or two, but the delivery was very slow, and sadly when the baby boy finally came, he was stillborn. To add to the family's grief, Dr. Martin said that Velma would not be able to deliver children and that there was no need to try again.

Elizabeth, as you remember, lived in Waycross, and she had heard of a doctor who could deliver a baby by caesarean which was not very common back in 1939. Asa Jr. and Velma really wanted a child so they made an appointment with Dr. Pomersey to get his opinion and see if it was possible for them to have a child. Upon examination the doctor concluded that they could have a child, but it would require a caesarean birth and could only be done once. If they wanted additional children they would have to adopt. They were warned that this was an expensive way to deliver a child, and that recovery would be long because the procedure was an invasive operation.

Asa Jr. went to see Asa Sr. and explain the situation to him. He hoped his pa would give him the money for the procedure. Asa Jr. told him they only had two choices, the cesarean birth or an adoption from the Baptist Children's Home. Asa Sr. didn't have to consider the options long.

He said "Okay we'll try this doctor's idea, because I want bloodline children to inherit from me." It was settled.

Within a few months Velma was pregnant again. They had to visit Dr. Pomersey every month initially and then every two weeks after six months. Of course Velma, already being spoiled and controlling, took full advantage of all the attention. She demanded, and got, a black housekeeper to do all the cooking and cleaning. She did not want Asa Jr. to go fishing or hunting with his cousins because, having never gotten over her insecure jealousies, she was afraid he would find a woman and have an affair.

In August Dr. Pomersey said it was time and admitted Velma to the hospital to prepare for the cesarean. It was performed on August 7, 1939, and was a success. The result was a healthy baby boy named Asa III. Both Grandpa and Pa were pleased that the family name would be carried on for another generation.

After a week the doctor said both mother and baby could go home, but Velma was told that she must be careful and must come back in two weeks for a check up and to have the stitches removed. Dr. Pomersey also required that she go home by ambulance. At this time in South Georgia, the ambulance was the hearse at the funeral home. It served the dual purpose of transporting dead bodies as well as living patients. The hearse from Thomas Funeral Home was sent to Waycross to take Velma and Asa III home.

When they got home, Aunt Polly was there to assist Velma with the baby. The baby was bottle fed on formula. The bottles used were glass and both the bottles and nipples had to be boiled in water to sterilize them. Sterilization was extremely important because infant mortality was high due to infection and illness. Velma was terrified that the baby would catch something and die like her younger sister and brother had, one from bronchial phenomena and the other from diphtheria. Of course immunization vaccines were limited with far fewer than we have today. Asa III's parents did make sure that he had all the shots that were available at the time, and they took every precaution they could to prevent disease and infection.

With the birth of Asa III, it looked as if the dynasty of the timber and land baron was assured. Life settled into the same old pace as before, and the family remained split into factions. Ma and Inez had little or nothing to do with Asa Jr. and Velma. Elizabeth, however, was on great terms with both sides of the family. Velma did not care for any of Asa Jr.'s family and insisted that they have more to do with her relatives because she felt they were more God fearing and therefore better people. It was her opinion that Asa Jr.'s kin were all wild, and whether this was true or not, she tended to instill this opinion into the mind of Asa III as well. Of course all three of Asa Sr.'s children from his first marriage to Ada continued to refuse to have anything to do with his second wife and their children.

TWENTY FIVE
Explosion

There was still a great demand for navel store products in the 1940s, especially during WWII, and so the farm and naval store businesses continued to be profitable. With additional land purchases and growing business profits, Asa Sr.'s worth kept increasing, as did his standing in the community.

It was at this time that some of Asa Sr.'s friends encouraged him to run for State Representative to the Georgia Assembly. Since he knew lots of folks and had generously helped many, he thought that he just might win, and so he got qualified to run and immediately began his campaign. Asa Jr. supported him by driving him all over the county to talk to voters.

One night during the campaign, Asa Jr. and Velma were awakened by a great explosion. They ran out onto the front porch and were shocked to see the turpentine still blazing. The drums with mineral spirits in them were exploding. The wooden shingles on the building were flying in the air and were like little torches ready to set anything on fire where they landed. Thankfully the wind was blowing them away from the quarters so no houses burned. However, these flaming projectiles caught the grist mill on fire, and others landed on the corn crib at the barn right across the street from Asa Jr. and Velma's house.

Jumping into action, they were able to extinguish it before it could take the crib and barn.

The explosion was heard for miles, and soon a crowd had gathered. Asa Jr. and some of the tenants were keeping a close lookout to make sure none of the flying burning shingles caught the commissary, any of the barns, or the gas station at the commissary on fire.

Asa Sr. arrived on the scene quickly, having heard the explosion at his house some two miles away. When it was over, fortunately the destruction was limited to the grist mill and still which had burned to the ground. The blaze was considered an accident, but there was unproven suspicion that maybe this was not the case. As soon as the rubble cooled enough, Asa Sr. put the turpentine hands to work cleaning up. In about two months they had rebuilt the still and had it in full operation again. Asa Sr. loved the turpentine still. He sat beside it a while every day, so its loss had been especially hard for him.

When it seemed that everything was restored and running smoothly, there was another fire in the middle of the night. This time it was the truck house that burned with the trucks in it. Of course there were more explosions from the gas tanks. This fire was so hot that the long steel frame to the transfer truck was warped and bent to the ground. The transfer truck was the one that hauled mineral spirits and rosin to Savannah, so replacing it immediately was crucial to keeping the business operating.

After the second fire, suspicions about the origin of both fires grew. Many believed then that they had been set by Asa Sr.'s political enemies, and then, to his great disappointment, he lost the election. The loss was believed to be partly due to his nasty divorce and the lawsuits it brought as well as his wealth. Besides his 10,000 acres, Asa Sr. had grown his business operation to the point that he went into partnership in another navel store operation in Denton. It was also thriving. Jealousy is an ugly creature, and Asa Sr. had worked hard to go from a woods rider to one of the wealthiest men in the county. Not everybody liked that.

TWENTY SIX

End of a Dynasty

After his business fires and his election loss, Asa Sr. never seemed quite the same. He was troubled that his first and second families had never overcome their animosities. Even after Asa Sr. and his second wife Lillie had another son, relations with his older children did not improve. They still insisted on referring to the boys from his marriage to Lillie as "the bastard children by the bitch." This hurt Asa Sr. deeply because they were after all, all his family.

When Asa Sr. began having trouble urinating, Dr. Martin sent him to see Dr. Revas, a specialist in Waycross, Georgia, who told him he had an enlarged prostrate and that it would have to be removed. In 1948 there was no other treatment available. Dr. Revas had previously operated successfully on several cousins for kidney stones and prostate problems. The surgery was scheduled for the following week, and since any surgery was serious business, Asa Sr. got his will in order just in case something went wrong during the operation.

Lillie and Alvin took Asa Sr. to Waycross for the surgery on Monday. The procedure was scheduled for Tuesday morning, but was delayed until the afternoon. In the operating room they gave Asa Sr. a shot to thicken his blood. Things seemed to be going well, but some clots formed. One went straight to his heart and another to his brain. Asa Sr. died on the operating table. No one had expected that!

Lillie and Alvin solemnly returned home. Alvin went to Asa Jr.'s house to tell him that his pa had died from blood clot to the heart and brain. Then Alvin said, "I'm going to town to get Thomas Funeral Home to pick up the body. Tomorrow we'll have to make funeral arrangements."

By mid-morning the next day, the news had spread throughout the community. There was great shock in both the white and Negro quarters as well as with all the family. Everybody who had depended on Asa Sr. for their livelihoods wondered what would happen now. The family was left wondering how things would go on without their strong patriarch.

Alvin, Asa Jr., and Lillie went to town to the funeral home to make the arrangements. It helped that Asa Jr. got along with Lillie better then the rest of the family. Together they picked out a bronze coffin with gold mounts, the most expensive one available because they all felt Asa Sr. should be honored with the best. It had a glass cover over the exposed part of the body rather than the usual netting. This was before air condition controlled environments, and so the covering protected the exposed part of the body from flies and other insects that were part of southern Georgia's humid climate.

It was traditional to have the body brought home to lie in state. People still sat up with the body all night long or 24 hours a day until the funeral. Asa Sr.'s funeral was scheduled for Saturday at Satilla Firewall Baptist Church. The body was brought home on Thursday afternoon, and because Asa Sr.'s death had been on the local radio and in the "Savannah News", there was already a crowd at the house when the body arrived.

The coffin was placed in front of the fireplace in the parlor which adjoined the dining room. The family went in to view the body, and after that the glass was put in place in the coffin. The coffin blanket had orchids with purple throats, one for each of the five children and the widow.

The guest book was put out for signing, and the crowd outside began filing in to pay their last respects. Later in the afternoon flowers began arriving, and by dark the parlor was filling up with a variety of flowers, sprays, and wreaths. There was picture molding in both the parlor and dining room, and the funeral director started hanging the sprays on them. Soon both rooms were full of flowers, and the house and porch were filled with people until late that night. Many followed the custom of staying up all night with the body.

The kitchen was full of generous amounts of food from the neighbors and church ladies. Offerings included fried chicken, fried steak, hams, potato salad, deviled eggs, beans squash, pickles, cakes, pies, banana pudding, and home- made biscuits. Folks saw that nobody went hungry.

With the exception of the Negros, most people who were going to the funeral came to the house to follow the hearse to the church and cemetery. When the hearse pulled out with the coffin for the three mile trip to the church, the last cars left the house as the hearse arrived at the church. This was an amazing outpouring of love and respect. Despite his loss of the election, Asa Sr. was genuinely well liked and very respected in the county. The church yard was full of the black hands; the windows in the church were opened so those who were not able to get inside the church could hear the service.

When the church was full and the last cars had arrived from the house, the funeral director closed the coffin, which had been open since it arrived at the church. The Reverend Graham conducted the service, a Masonic funeral, and a soloist sang *When They Ring Them Golden Bells*. There was a lot of soft crying during the service, and when it was completed, the funeral director opened the casket again, a tradition in the South, so that everyone could file by for one last good bye.

Those in the church filed past first, followed by those outside, and then all of the Negros, most of them sobbing because their boss was gone, and they had loved him. Asa Sr. had been progressive and forward thinking and had always been good to them.

Lastly, the family passed by the coffin. Lillie fainted, as did Inez. Two of Asa Sr.'s sisters nearly passed out as well, but the funeral director was prepared with smelling salts. After all of the family had their final viewing, the coffin was closed. The pallbearers carried it to the cemetery, with the family following, to the family plot Asa Sr. had purchased.

After the coffin was lowered into the vault, the throngs of folks left. The family returned later when the flowers were arranged on the grave. Each representative orchid was then taken by a family member to be pressed and kept as a memento of the funeral, a cherished final connection to Asa Stall, Sr. With his passing it was the end of an era.

Within two years the turpentine still and commissary were closed. The land was split between the heirs. All that was left were the splinters of a once great business built by a south Georgia woods rider who became a great timber and land baron.

Acknowledgments

I would like to thank the following people, without whose assistance, this book would not have been happened.

Jennifer Newton, my Administrative Assistant, for her help with the original manuscript, especially hours of typing it from my longhand notes

Margaret Pomeroy for bringing the manuscript to fruition with her editing and publishing skills

Joseph Bennett, my partner, for support, encouragement, enthusiasm, and many hours of reading